S0-DZN-017

Disappeared!

Disappeared!

Technique of Terror

A Report for the Independent Commission on International Humanitarian Issues

Zed Books Ltd
London and New Jersey

This report does not necessarily reflect the views, individually or collectively, of the members of the Independent Commission on International Humanitarian Issues (ICIHI). It is based on research carried out for ICIHI and was prepared under the supervision of its Secretariat with the guidance of the ICIHI Working Group on Refugees and Displaced People.

Disappeared! was first published by Zed Books Ltd.,
57 Caledonian Road, London N1 9BU and
171 First Avenue, Atlantic Highlands, New Jersey 07716, in 1986.

© Secretariat of the Independent Commission on International
Humanitarian Issues, 1986

Cover design by Henry Iles
Cover photograph by Jean Mohr
Typeset by Grassroots Typeset, London
Printed and bound in Great Britain by
Cox & Wyman Ltd., Reading

All rights reserved

British Library Cataloguing in Publication Data

Disappeared!: technique of terror: a report.
1. Political prisoners 2. Missing persons
3. Assassination
I. Independent Commission on International
Humanitarian Issues
365'.45   HV8963

ISBN 0-86232-698-2
ISBN 0-86232-699-0 Pbk

Contents

The Independent Commission on International Humanitarian Issues

Co-Chairmen:
Sadruddin Aga Khan (Iran)   Hassan bin Talal (Jordan)

Members:

Susanna Agnelli	(Italy)
Talal Bin Abdul Aziz Al Saud	(Saudi Arabia)
Paulo Evaristo Arns, Vice-Chairman	(Brazil)
Mohammed Bedjaoui	(Algeria)
Henrik Beer, Treasurer	(Sweden)
Luis Echeverria Alvarez	(Mexico)
Pierre Graber	(Switzerland)
Ivan Head	(Canada)
M. Hidayatullah	(India)
Aziza Hussein	(Egypt)
Manfred Lachs	(Poland)
Robert McNamara	(USA)
Lazar Mojsov	(Yugoslavia)
Mohamed Mzali, Vice-Chairman	(Tunisia)
Sadako Ogata, Vice-Chairman	(Japan)
David Owen	(United Kingdom)
Willibald P. Pahr, Vice-Chairman	(Austria)
Shridath S. Ramphal	(Guyana)
Ru Xin	(China)
Salim A. Salim	(Tanzania)
Léopold Sédar Senghor	(Senegal)
Soedjatmoko	(Indonesia)
Desmond Tutu	(South Africa
Simone Veil	(France)
Gough Whitlam	(Australia)

Secretary General, ex-officio member:
Zia Rizvi (Pakistan)

Other ICIHI Reports*

FAMINE: A Man-Made Disaster? (Pan Books, London/Sydney, 1985). Other language editions: Arabic, French, Italian, Japanese, Portuguese, Serbo-Croatian, Spanish and Urdu.

STREET CHILDREN: A Growing Urban Tragedy (Weidenfeld & Nicolson, London, 1986). Other language editions: Arabic, French, Indonesian, Japanese, Serbo-Croatian and Spanish.

THE ENCROACHING DESERT: The Consequences of Human Failure (Zed Books, London/New Jersey, 1986 and College Press, Harare, 1986). Other language editions: Arabic and French.

THE VANISHING FOREST: The Human Consequences of Deforestation (Zed Books, London/New Jersey, 1986 and College Press, Harare, 1986). Other language editions: French and Serbo-Croatian.

REFUGEES: The Dynamics of Displacement (Zed Books, London/New Jersey, 1986). Other language editions: Arabic, French and Japanese.

MODERN WARS: The Humanitarian Challenge (Zed Books, London/New Jersey, 1986). Other language editions: French and Japanese.

Other reports to be published include:
  Statelessness
  Autochthonous People
  Mass Expulsions
  Disaster Management
  Displaced Persons
  Protection of Children
  The Urban Child: Perspectives and Problems
  Urban Migration
  New Man-Made Disasters

* in addition to the Commission's Final Report.

ICIHI Working Group on Disappeared Persons

The following members of the Independent Commission helped in the preparation of this Report in their individual capacities:

Sadruddin Aga Khan	(Iran)
Paulo Evaristo Arns	(Brazil)
Mohammed Bedjaoui	(Algeria)
Simone Veil	(France)

Drafting Committee

Zia Rizvi	Mohamed El Kouhene
(Co-ordinator)	Pierre Spitz
	(Editors)

Introduction

Disappeared! The reader may well find such a title somewhat surprising. Who has disappeared? Why should the Independent Commission on International Humanitarian Issues think it necessary to address the subject and publish its conclusions in this Report?

To avoid any risk of ambiguity, it should be made clear from the outset that those to whom the title refers are not among the many people who every year decide to exchange one life, and perhaps one identity, for another. Nor are they victims of criminal acts whose bodies are never recovered.

The disappeared persons whose cause the Commission decided to uphold and whom the international community as a whole should defend are the men, women, and children who are deliberately made to disappear for political reasons.

It might be felt that this issue is too narrow and too hazy to justify a special study. The importance given to this method of repression, used systematically by certain totalitarian or authoritarian regimes, nonetheless justifies alerting world opinion. It must be condemned unequivocally and ways must be sought to prevent it, just like other abuses which have long featured in the sad list of the violations of human rights explicitly forbidden by international conventions and declarations.

Enforced disappearance is repression in a new guise. It is still largely unknown to the general public. It is hard for the friends and relatives of the victims to denounce, and has so far been little studied by legal experts. It combines in itself violations of several fundamental rights: the right to freedom, the right to physical integrity, and usually the right to life. Disappearance also violates all rights of legal defence,

13

since no warrant for arrest is issued; there is no trial, no defending advocate and no public announcement.

For those who order disappearances or those who, by their acquiescence, are its silent accomplices, the technique is extremely 'efficient' and 'convenient': there is no evidence, and no proof, which guarantees immunity from international condemnation and from any internal protest. This characteristic explains why, at a time when the international community is increasingly well-informed and vigilant, totalitarian or authoritarian governments wishing to preserve the appearance of democracy—because they are dependent on a particular great power and fear possible reprisals—entrust military or paramilitary forces with the task of making their political opponents, real or imaginary, disappear. Witnesses to the event and even individuals singled out at random, so as to intimidate the whole population and deter it from any thought of resistance, are themselves at risk.

Mention of political disappearances commonly brings to mind certain countries in Latin America. The regimes in question have, indeed, found in it an effective instrument which allows them to preserve the veneer of respectability they need *vis-à-vis* the outside world. It is this requirement that determines the subtle balance between maintaining the rule of law (however qualified), which can lead foreign opinion and even part of the domestic population to think that fundamental freedoms are preserved, and the reality of a regime which represses through the use of terror the activities of its opponents. Despite the authoritarian and repressive character of these regimes, their wish or need for a respectable façade explains the existence of opposition parties. These, in turn, secretly keep the outside world informed of the reality.

While resolutely denouncing crimes perpetrated in such countries in the name of public order and liberal economic policies, it would be a dangerous error not to recognize that the gravest violations of human rights are those which cannot even be denounced because the population lives under a reign of terror, because all potential dissidents are systematically eliminated and because contacts with the outside world are practically impossible.

Examples from the relatively recent past demand that one should be careful about passing judgement on a particular regime according to criteria which are only relevant to the democratic countries which respect them. Appearances can be deceptive, especially when the yardstick of effectiveness in political repression is the capacity to discourage or block any temptation to resist.

How can one forget the tacit approval given to Nazi Germany by many visitors, not all of whom were necessarily sympathetic, and even by certain organizations, blinded or subdued by the orderliness and the courtesy they met with everywhere? And yet, while the 1936 Olympic Games were being held in Berlin for athletes from all over the world, Jews and political opponents were being exterminated in Dachau.

A shroud of silence had fallen over the German people, only to be lifted after the fall of the Nazi state.

In the Soviet Union, it took Khruschev's report to the Party for the existence of the Gulag to be acknowledged.

Ten months after the capture of Phnom Penh by the Khmer Rouge, nothing was known about what was happening in Cambodia. The fate of millions who disappeared during the upheavals of revolution and countless others was sealed in silence.

There are reasons to believe, however, that in future, whatever the means at their disposal, dictatorships will find it more and more difficult to conceal phenomena on this scale. The international community is becoming more vigilant and journalists are now less and less hesitant to take risks when reporting and gathering evidence on suspect countries.

This is why regimes anxious to preserve appearances now prefer to make people who are potential threats disappear, purely and simply. They deny all responsibility and painstakingly remove all traces of the evidence.

Any approach to the subject dictates a measure of caution, however, and an awareness of inherent limitations. Evaluation of disappearances is difficult by the nature of things; a wide margin of error is the norm. Whereas information circulates relatively easily in cities, the same is not true of rural areas. In places where fighting is taking place between guerrillas and government troops, responsibility for certain cases of disappearance may be hard to pinpoint. Repressive forces are not the only ones to use the blackmail of terror: resistance movements, more or less organized, can equally well be dragged into the cycle of violence.

How can one ignore the fact that similar situations, and the resulting confusion, encourage the emergence of acts of pure banditry? The simplicity and advantages of such methods lead one to fear that, in some regimes, disappearances can become standard practice, the final but officially unrecognized 'solution'.

When the victims are silenced and when family and friends face endless obstacles and difficulties, it is more than ever vital that those who are free should echo and amplify their cries through the desolation of fear and indifference.

Although the will to resist of those in the front line has been expressed by several non-governmental organizations, world public opinion is not yet sufficiently aware of this new danger which looms over human rights.

In presenting this report, the Independent Commission hopes to make a useful contribution to the defence of those whose rights and very lives are threatened by their struggle in the cause of liberty.

Simone Veil

Editorial Note

Disappearances, a sinister form of political repression, were first documented in the mid-70s. Since then, greater awareness of the widespread use of clandestine abductions and torture to terrorize and silence opponents has helped expose the various regimes which attempt to cloak their abuse of human rights in secrecy and anonymity.

Such practices rightly provoke our loudest condemnation. Their impact on victims, their families, and society as a whole has, from the outset, been accorded high priority by the Independent Commission. At its first Plenary Meeting, the Commission heard numbing testimony from those directly affected by this inhuman practice. Their accounts sadly underlined the necessity of more concrete and effective action at the national and international level.

This Report, which is dedicated to the memory of all those who have disappeared, is based on detailed discussions with human rights workers and individuals who have been actively involved in combating disappearances or have suffered, directly or indirectly, from this insidious practice. The Report also reflects the discussions which took place during several plenary sessions of the Independent Commission as well as its Working Group on Disappearances under the chairmanship of Madame Simone Veil.

The preparation of this Report is due in no small part to the courage and integrity of many individuals who must remain anonymous. Those who contributed actively to the preparation of this Report are too numerous to mention, but the Commission would particularly like to thank Mrs Casal de Ghatti, of Uruguay, whose husband, pregnant daughter and son-in-law disappeared; Mr Hipolito Solari Yrigoyen, former Vice-President of the Argentinian Senate, who himself 'disappeared' but was subsequently released; the 'Grandmothers of the Plaza de Mayo'; and the writer, the late Julio Cortazar, whose commitment to the cause of human rights is widely known and respected.

Special thanks are due to K. Herndl, Assistant Secretary-General of the United Nations and Director of the UN Centre for Human Rights; I. Tosevski, Chairman of the Working Group on Enforced or Involuntary Disappearances of the United Nations Human Rights Commission; G. Mauntner-Markhof of the United Nations Centre for Human Rights; L. Despouy and L. Joinet, experts of the Sub-Commission against Discrimination and the Protection of Minorities, A. Bentoumi, Secretary-General of the International Association of Democratic Lawyers, H. Taviani, President of Terre d'Asile; P. Rice, Executive Secretary of FEDEFAM; C. Dominicé, of the International Committee of the Red Cross; A Artucio of the International Committee of Jurists; C. Desormeaux of Amnesty International; and R.-P. Paringaux of *Le Monde*. The Commission would also like to express its gratitude to the United Nations Organization, the Council of Europe, the Arab League, the Organization of American States and the Organization of African Unity, whose documentation has been most valuable.

The Commission wishes to record its grateful appreciation to M. El Kouhene and P. Spitz whose enthusiasm and competence contributed so much to the preparation of this Report. The English translation was done by T. B. Meyer. The technical preparation was greatly facilitated by M. Fall, F. Frank and N. Niland.

We would also like to thank R. Molteno of Zed Books for his valuable support in arranging the publication of the Report.

Any income from the sale of this book will be devoted entirely to research on humanitarian issues.

S. Veil
Convenor
ICIHI Working Group on
Disappeared Persons

Z. Rizvi
Secretary General

Geneva, July 1986.

1. Suspended Mourning

*Grief has limits, whereas
apprehension has none. For we
grieve only for what we know has
happened, but we fear all that
possibly may happen.*

Gaius Plinius, c.97-110

Some men arrive. They force their way into a family's home, rich
or poor, house, hovel or hut, in a city or in a village, anywhere.
They come at any time of the day or night, usually in plain clothes,
sometimes in uniform, always carrying weapons. Giving no
reasons, producing no arrest warrant, without saying who they are
or on whose authority they are acting, they drag off one or more
members of the family towards a car, using violence in the process
if necessary.

Once the commotion is over, those left behind can only wonder.
They have heard people say: these things happen, that those who
are taken away are never seen again. Who were these men? Why
didn't they show any papers as the police always do when they
arrest a suspect, be it for petty theft or a horrible crime? Why?

Such, very often, is the first act of the drama. There can, of
course, be other scenarios. The abduction may occur at the work-
place, in front of colleagues who can warn the family. Or on official
premises, like a hospital, where pressure by the authorities will
make first-hand reports unlikely. It may take place in the city or
in the countryside. The person simply does not return home at the
usual time. Anxiety turns to anguish; there are rumours, and maybe
the first reports from witnesses.

The search for information follows a similar pattern in every
country concerned—with the police, local authorities, and the law;
in prisons, barracks and special detention centres. The answers are
always the same—no, we don't know, there's nobody by that name
listed here. Sometimes, with luck, and presence of mind, someone

may have noted the car number plate, which may facilitate the identification of the police station or the military unit involved. But they will still deny any involvement—the car must have been stolen, or sold, or the number changed.

For those who are searching for a member of their family or one of their acquaintances who has disappeared, the path always leads through uncertainty, denials, and lies by the authorities. What varies is the degree of legal assistance available, which depends on the maturity of the legal system, the courage of the lawyers in the face of the risks they run, the financial resources available, and in particular the morale of the families concerned. There are also variations in the degree and type of threats exercised by the authorities against those undertaking the search.

Those who are abducted—men or women—wonder not only about their own fate, but also worry about their families and their friends. How are they living? Are they being threatened? Can they help? Messages and letters remain unanswered. As the victims of the abduction become aware of their isolation, they realize that a new term exists to define their status: 'disappeared'.

The term was first used in a specific sense by human rights organizations and the Latin American media in 1974, and was later adopted in other parts of the world. The technique of enforced disappearance is by no means new. Repressive governments have always been tempted to get rid of troublesome opponents, and have often succeeded in doing so. In its 1986 Report, the United Nations Working Group on Enforced or Involuntary Disappearances (see Chapter 4) noted that, during the previous year, the phenomenon is known to have occurred in at least 36 countries. [1]

Disappearances are a doubly lethal form of torture, for the victims who are kept ignorant of their fate, and for family members who wait and wonder, and may never receive any news. And the victims know that their families are unaware of their whereabouts. Having disappeared from society, their only mental bearings are within their own minds or within the walls of their place of detention. If death is not the final outcome and they are eventually released from the nightmare, the victims may suffer from the psychological consequences of this form of dehumanization for a long time. Such effects cannot be specifically identified, as it is difficult to distinguish those resulting from the disappearance itself from those caused by the brutality and torture which usually accompany it.

The family and friends of disappeared persons are also subjected to slow mental torture—not knowing whether the victim is still alive and, if so, where, and in what state of health, and under what conditions? And knowing, furthermore, that they too are threatened, that they can expect the same fate themselves, that to search for the truth is itself dangerous.

If my son had been killed in an accident, I would know he was dead, I would have buried him, and with time—you don't forget, you can't forget—yet you try to accept that it was God's will. But they got him in the street, he was beaten up, and nobody has seen him since. It's dreadful not knowing if he has anything to eat, or if he's cold, or has a place to sleep. How can I bear to think that my son is in the hands of that crowd of crooks, to think of what they might be doing to him. Can you understand how a mother feels?

This type of distress is frequently compounded by the material circumstances accompanying the disappearance—unemployment, loss of income, and the costs incurred in the search. For while the family's deepest emotions are gravely affected, they suffer equally in economic terms. The complete uncertainty over the timing of the victim's ever hoped-for return makes it difficult to adapt to the new situation. If the father and wage-earner disappears, the mother must find employment of some kind to compensate. Her task is frequently hampered by the family being ostracized and by employers' fears of getting into trouble themselves. The fear of 'guilt by association' often prevails over solidarity. Economic and social marginalization are mutually reinforcing. Failure to find alternative employment increases economic deprivation, and the family slips inexorably into the ranks of the most deprived.

If a job can be found, the time it takes up cuts into the time needed for the search and for the procedures involved in finding the disappeared person. There is little time left for the children. If they are very fortunate, they can continue living in their normal surroundings. Sometimes they will be obliged to live elsewhere, for example with their grandparents.

Occasionally, the older children take over responsibility for running the household and care for their younger brothers and sisters. Some may even start working. They are obliged to leave school and abandon plans for the future due to their new role and the

21

change in their lives.

Day after day, month after month, in an atmosphere of psychological stress, economic difficulties and social deprivation, the father's, mother's, or parents' absence is deeply felt. The children seek explanations. They need to be comforted, for a child who witnesses a violent arrest and abduction will not easily forget it. The violence may be associated with images, noises and emotions, in different combinations, which may profoundly affect them, such as strangers bursting into the house, a door being forced open, or shouts in the night which tear them from their sleep. Roughly handled, insulted, injured in some cases, and powerless before the humiliation of their parents, these children have often witnessed brutality, even torture.

The Abandoned Child Syndrome

In these circumstances, the results of a survey[2] carried out in Chile on 203 children under 12 years of age, one or both of whose parents had disappeared, are hardly surprising. Physical and psychological testing (by interview, drawings, Goodenough tests, etc.) showed that 78% of those examined exhibited symptoms of withdrawal; 70% suffered from depression. Other symptoms included intense and generalized fear, triggered by specific stimuli such as sirens, the sight of men in uniform and the noise of a car at night (78%); loss of weight and appetite, disturbed sleep, decline in general behaviour and in scholastic aptitude, and increased dependence on adults, particularly the mother (in approximately 50% of cases).

The younger the children, the more serious their condition. The severity of the symptoms varies according to their age, the duration of the trauma, the extent of social isolation, and the degree to which they have found the explanation for the parent's absence convincing. Most of the children in the survey (65%) were under six years of age. If they were told the truth they did not always find it acceptable, but lies and half-truths were even more disturbing. The removal of one or several members of a family, combined with social and economic deprivation, typically produces alternating phases of hope and despair which are emotionally draining for everyone concerned and make normal development of the child impossible. As one family member said: 'The future is just a blank. There is no legal precedent: we have no right of appeal to anyone. We are in limbo, hanging between life and death'.

Surveys of other groups of children have been carried out in Chile, Mexico (children of Argentine refugees), and Canada (children of Chilean refugees). Over half of the 28 Argentine children[3] had witnessed forced entry into their homes, followed by breakages and looting, and seen violence and even torture practised on their parents. In 1979, 25% of these children were still deprived of one parent by imprisonment, death or disappearance. One third of their number had been separated from their parents before joining them in exile. Others had lived in prison with their parents, or had been born there, under conditions of extreme overcrowding and a total lack of hygiene.

These children showed symptoms of personality disorders, a serious cause for concern for their future. According to the educational staff, therapists and psychiatrists of the Integral Support Group in Buenos Aires, damage to the child's emotional and psychological development is particularly serious when the trauma produced by the mother's disappearance occurs during the first year of life.[4] This group examined and treated 62 children of disappeared persons. All of them felt that they had been abandoned. In the most severe cases, this feeling was evidenced by a withdrawal from the outside world and lowered levels of perception, even to the extent of staring fixedly into space.

In children aged between five and seven at the time of the abduction, behavioral changes are not irreversible. According to Drs. Mirta Guarino and Norberto Liwski, who worked with the Integral Support Group, the psychological condition in such cases may be considerably improved by appropriate attention in the family circle and by strong supportive therapy including talking to the child, playing games, etc.

Clearly, this type of remedial action was only made possible by the change of government in Argentina, which brought the truth about disappearances to light, and put an end to the marginalization of the families concerned. It is significant that, once the process of political normalization had begun, the large number and high quality of social workers, doctors, psychologists and psychiatrists in the country made it relatively easy to establish a number of highly skilled working groups. In other countries, less well equipped, it

23

is impossible to provide the same standard of treatment for children suffering from this form of trauma once the situation is restored to normal. Solidarity provided by extended families and supportive communities (such as in Africa), however, may to some extent help the child overcome his or her difficulties. The longer the return to normality is delayed, the more the child's development will, inevitably, be perturbed.

In children of school age, the Argentinian doctors of the Integral Support Group have identified several negative symptoms in the normal process of social development, in their school work (lack of interest, difficulties in concentrating, and emotional crises which make even the simplest tasks impossible), and at the psychomotor level (difficulties of co-ordination, inhibition, aggressiveness, insecurity). They also noted that the older children saw the state as threatening rather than protective. For many adolescents, the manifest breakdown of the legal system justifies taking the law into their own hands.

A Broken World

In the eyes of the victims' children, the violent, treacherous and cowardly practice of abduction legitimizes the use of violence. It splits the family unit apart, in a manner beyond their understanding, and makes dialogue between parents and children impossible for an indefinite period. It destroys the normal framework and reference points of personality development in quite a different way from other types of trauma. There are two reasons for this: the lack of any convincing explanation, and diminished social solidarity.

Mutual support is, of course, particularly strong in wartime. The child is given a clear explanation of why the father is away. As in the case of disappearances, the duration of the absence due to war is indefinite. Perhaps he will never return. It may be very difficult, or impossible, to receive or send news to the missing parent. Yet this situation is acceptable to the entire community. It is valued, perhaps even overvalued, by society as a whole because the father is said to be defending his country and, by extension, all those living there, including his own family. General solidarity of this kind is also forthcoming in material terms.

Limited support is often also available in certain cases of persecution, especially when the target is relatively specific, for example when the parents belong to a particular political, religious or ethnic group. This attachment allows for a convincing explanation, thus reinforcing identity with the group. It can increase determination to defend it, and even incite the members to avenge those who have been harmed. The child may also receive help and sympathy from outside the group. During World War II, for example, many Jewish children in Europe were taken in by non-Jewish families.

In the case of disappearances, the impressions the child receives from his family, from the neighbourhood and at school are varied, or even contradictory. They oscillate between two extremes—criticism for what may have been the reason for the disappearance (political opinions, imprudence, etc.), or its idealization. In this case, the child feels cut off from the rest of the family and loses his bearings between these conflicting attitudes. The family group also tends to withdraw into itself to 'protect' the child from what others may say. Others within the community tend to accentuate this form of exclusion further so long as repression lasts.

The closest analogy to the position of children of disappeared persons is that of abandoned children. But it is forced abandonment, since it is against the parents' wishes and desires. For even the child of the most hardened criminal may visit his father in prison or correspond with him. Even when the details of the crime are kept hidden, the child is vaguely aware that social norms have been broken. In normal everyday life, a crime is a crime, a prison a prison, a death a death. In the world of disappearances, on the other hand, everything is mysterious and enigmatic, anything may be true or false. Society, authority and justice contradict each other.

The way the children of victims see the world gives a clearer insight into the perverse nature of this form of persecution.

Independently of their perceptions, however, their state of health is also revealing. In Argentina, doctors attached to the Integral Support Group found the children of disappeared persons in a very poor state of health, the result of a combination of mutually reinforcing physical and psychological factors. Diagnosis of a group of 62 children showed that 92% suffered from symptoms caused by wounds and injuries, 63% from intestinal disorders (diarrhoea), 22% from bronchitis, etc. One figure in particular attracted their attention—86% of the sample required dental care. Why? In a country like Argentina, where the standard of living and dietary habits of the urban population are similar to those in an industrialized country, regular dental care is a necessity, but is not easily accepted by children. Active parental involvement is required for the periodic treatment of tooth decay and regular dental care. In the absence of parental supervision, especially when numerous and far more serious problems are constantly present, dental care is neglected and check-ups are postponed until 'later'. This highlights the specific character of disappearances: uncertainty, more waiting, and the hope that things will return to normal—tomorrow, or the day after tomorrow, or perhaps next month. For the family of the disappeared person, life grinds to a standstill.

Concealed Births

One of the most sinister aspects of the practice of enforced disappearance is the abduction of pregnant women. The pregnancy is allowed to reach full term, unless prison conditions and the maltreatment inflicted on the victim terminate it prematurely; the baby is then taken away from the mother shortly after birth. Since the mother is not legally a prisoner, the same applies to the child, who may therefore be handed over to a childless couple. After faking a few documents with the help of the authorities, the couple declares the child as their own. Alternatively, the anonymous child is confined to an institution, abandoned, sold, or killed.

A number of eye-witness reports on the subject collected in Argentina by Amnesty International and CONADEP (the National Commission on the Disappearance of Persons, established by the Argentine Government) are now available, as are statements made during the trial of nine former members of the military junta. These sources reveal that, while pregnant women were not spared torture, they were generally allowed to give birth before being transferred elsewhere or killed.

The Escuela Mecánica de la Armada (ESMA), the principal naval engineering college in Buenos Aires, was used as a detention centre for abducted prisoners. The following account concerning the birth of children to women who were pregnant at the time of their abduction by the security forces comes from three women detainees:[5]

When we arrived at ESMA, we were taken to a part of the building known as 'Capucha' (the hood). Many of the women there were pregnant. Their condition did not prevent them from being tortured. The scars could be seen on their bodies.

The fate of the mother and child was sealed on arrival. The mother was destined for 'transfer', the child for an uncertain future. The child could never be entrusted to its family, for it would have been living proof of what had happened to the mother. The naval hospital had a list of couples working in the Navy who were unable to have children of their own, and were willing to adopt the children of prisoners who had died or disappeared. It was in the hands of a gynaecologist in the hospital.

Sometimes the women gave birth in ordinary hospitals or were attended by midwives or civilian doctors who felt obliged by their conscience to inform the families concerned of the victims' whereabouts. In some cases, this led to their own abduction or 'disappearance'.

One midwife, D., attended the premature birth of twins to the 'disappeared' prisoner R.; two fair-haired boys were born on 22 April 1977 in the Olmos Prison.[6] She sent news to the family of the two babies, who had been placed in intensive care. R. had been abducted in La Plata on 10 December 1976, when she was four months pregnant. On 17 May 1977, the family learned that the mother and children had been separated and sent to an unknown destination. The midwife's humane action resulted in her own abduction and that of her husband, Dr E., in August 1977. Four more names were thus added to the long list of those who had disappeared.

This case was investigated by the organization founded by the grandmothers of disappeared children in Argentina (*Abuelas de Plaza de Mayo*). After extensive enquiries, it traced two children who were thought to be the twins. They were in the home of a police officer who claimed they were his own. In 1984, the putative grandparents instituted proceedings in La Plata. Judge B. of the Second Criminal Court ordered the analysis of blood samples from the grandparents and the police officer and his wife to determine their relationship to the children. These tests were scheduled for 31 January 1985, but the couple failed to appear or send the children. A communiqué issued by the police stated that the family was on holiday.

Disappeared!

It is interesting to note that various works of fiction which recreate the dramatic atmosphere of disappearances are now starting to appear, particularly in Latin America. One example is the recent Argentinian film, forceful yet sensitive, *Historia Oficial*, by Luis Puenzo, which describes the trauma involved in trying to locate children born in secret detention.

Mothers and children are separated for two reasons. Firstly, it increases the mother's suffering. This is not to exert additional pressure, but rather to punish her for being, in the eyes of her torturers, a real or imagined political dissident. The second reason was defined by the former chief of police for the province of Buenos Aires, who was subsequently gaoled. He was questioned about this practice by journalists in February 1984.[7] After denying that he had eliminated any children personally, he justified the separation of mothers and children by adding that 'Subversive parents teach their children to be subversive. That has got to stop'.

In pursuing its investigations, CONADEP asked the American Association for the Advancement of Science (AAAS) to send forensic experts to Argentina. By using genetic techniques, both in autopsies and on living tissue, they were able to verify relationships between living parents and children, dead and alive, and distinguish truth from allegation.

Sophisticated methods of this kind are not always available. Argentina is also one of the rare countries where a change in regime has put an end to terrorism by the State and allowed official investigations into what happened to take place.

In countries where the practice of disappearances persists, or is increasing, information is difficult to obtain and verify. It is, none the less, apparent that there are distinct similarities between the various physical and psychological consequences of disappearances, both for the victims themselves and for their relatives.

As evidenced by the details of the following case[8] reported by an Amnesty International team, which included a surgeon and a forensic pathologist, concerning the abduction and torture of a 26-year-old woman in Uganda, the date and country where a disappearance takes place are immaterial. Along with a dozen other people, K. was abducted by soldiers. She was with her two-year-old daughter at the time. Her son of six had managed to escape. After being subjected to brutality, torture and rape, she was separated from her daughter. K. managed to escape by bribing a soldier. She has not seen her daughter since and is unable to find out what happened to her.

Amid the variety of institutional arrangements and the range of different cultural values, economic and social conditions, and political regimes, the suffering caused by disappearances assumes a universal significance—like the despair of a child brutally separated from the family, like the anguish of suspended mourning.

Notes

1. Countries where disappearances are known to have occurred during 1985 are: Angola, Argentina, Bolivia, Brazil, Central African Republic, Chile, Colombia, Cyprus, Dominican Republic, El Salvador, Ethiopia, Guatemala, Guinea, Haiti, Honduras, Indonesia, Iran, Iraq, Lebanon, Mexico, Morocco, Nepal, Nicaragua, Paraguay, Peru, Philippines, Seychelles, South Africa (and Namibia), Sri Lanka, Syria, Togo, Uganda, Uruguay, Vietnam and Zaire.
   (E/CN4/1986/18)
2. F. Allodi, 'The psychiatric effects in children and families of victims of political persecution and torture', *Danish Medical Bulletin* . Vol. 27, Nov. 1980, pp. 229-231.
3. Ibid.
4. Mirta Guarino and Norberto Liwski, *Hijos de desaparecidos, secuelas del abandono forzado*, Ediciones del Movimiento Ecuménico por los Derechos Humanos. Libertad 257-1 A, 1012 Buenos Aires, 1983.
5. Amnesty International, *Les enfants disparus d'Argentine. Informations sur les enquêtes en cours*, Paris, 16 August 1985. (SF 85 CA 415/AMR 13-2-85), p. 6-7.
6. Ibid., p. 11.
7. Ibid., p. 3.
8. Amnesty International, *Ouganda, constat de torture*, Paris, June 1985. (SF 85 CA 33O/AFR 59-06-85), p. 30.

2. The New Face of Terror

The tyrant claims freedom to kill
  freedom
And yet to keep it for himself.

Rabindranath Tagore, 1928

The door of the car in which you are being taken away closes—
the first of the many doors which will divide you from your family
and your freedom. Where are you going? Is this an arrest or are
you being kidnapped? An arrest has the trappings of legality and
the rule of law; a kidnapping is at the whim of an individual.
Perhaps this arrest is meant to look like a kidnapping so as to
terrorize my family even more. In a moment they are going to take
me to an office, fill out some forms, and explain what I am being
held for. Then they will realize their mistake, I shall ask for a
lawyer and write to my family to reassure them.

We must imagine ourselves for a moment in the position of the
person, man or woman, undergoing such an ordeal. We know there
will be no forms to fill out, nor will there be legal procedures of
any kind. He will have no chance to communicate with the outside world, or to invoke, in his own defence, the humanitarian
principles accepted by human societies since time immemorial.

Indeed, the circumstances of the victim's detention only serve
to confirm the fears raised by the way in which he was abducted—
his fate is entirely arbitrary. There is no hope of getting a public
trial in open court, when the accused can at least proclaim his
innocence or, if he was arrested for holding unorthodox views,
defend his right to freedom of opinion. The case will not even be
heard *in camera*, when he could confront those who pass judgement. Words are stifled, cries go unheard, legally he or she doesn't
exist, and so cannot fight back by legal proceedings of any kind.
No hunger strike will draw attention to his protest. And if the person

31

finally dies in prison, the fact will not even be recorded, or the family informed. They will continue to hope and wait.

No justification is ever given for a disappearance since, by definition, the authorities deny it has occurred. Relatives, friends, neighbours and colleagues can only guess as to the reasons which prompted those responsible. Some victims may have been involved in activities considered by the authorities to be unacceptable, such as participating in trade unions or public demonstrations. Others disappear because their political opinions differ from the official line, or are held to be 'subversive'. Others, again, may be considered 'likely' to hold such views, or 'likely' to become political opponents. Still others may have been the object of slanderous or false statements made by private individuals, or may simply have been picked at random to maintain the reign of terror. Faceless terror.

P., a national of a country in Asia, was abducted by four members of a paramilitary organization on his way to the local market. They forced him into their car, and he has not been seen since. So far, all his family's efforts to find him have come to nothing. He was suspected of 'subversive activities'.

In a different continent, Africa, a stock breeder saw some men drive up to his home in a Land Rover. They claimed his sons were guerrillas, and asked him where they were. The farmer was violently beaten up with rifle butts, taken away, and never seen again.

A world away in Latin America, I., a doctor, married and the father of three children, was abducted by soldiers in uniform fifteen minutes after leaving his clinic. Witnesses saw him bundled into a car, which was later found abandoned. His wife put requests for information in the newspapers and started legal proceedings, but without success. She has no idea what happened to him.

In Europe, the armed conflict in 1974 between the Greek and Turkish communities in Cyprus was immediately followed by many cases of disappearances: 2,400 according to a United Nations estimate. While there is no evidence of other disappearances with government complicity in Europe on a similar scale, there have been other serious violations of human rights, including torture, political trials, and restrictions on personal freedom.

Regimes based on marxist ideology can generally be considered a special category with regard to disappearances. Although, in the initial turmoil following the seizure of power, those opposed to the new state of affairs may well be done away with in summary fashion, governments of this kind can generally avoid having to resort to the practice of disappearances as a matter of policy. While opposition to the government or merely holding non-conformist views may itself be an indictable offence, the violations of human rights involved cannot be termed disappearances so long as the authorities admit responsibility for their actions and the victims' families are aware of their whereabouts.

The total number of disappearances world-wide runs into thousands, and there are many different scenarios. Men, women and children disappear from one moment to the next; nobody knows where they are or what has become of them. Sometimes, after weeks, months, or years, victims of abduction reappear. They have either been released, or have managed to escape, or their relatives have found out where they are being held and have managed to arrange for their release, sometimes by paying a ransom. Their accounts of their abduction and the conditions of their imprisonment are terrifying, and tell of beatings, injuries, torture, rape, and the execution of other prisoners in their presence.

'They bound my hands and legs', recalls one woman, 'and tied me to a metal chair. The soldiers came and hung an old tyre above my head. They set fire to it and left me underneath. There were so many other prisoners in there, men and women. Drops of burning rubber fell on to my head, my face, my right hand and right breast. The pain was absolutely indescribable. I spent the whole day like that, from 8.30 in the morning onwards'.

One could quote many other forms of torture, of course, used against disappeared persons and other victims. The variety of methods employed bears witness to the viciousness of the persecution and the perverted imagination of cruel men.

What Is a 'Disappearance'?

A clear definition of the term 'disappearance' has more than merely theoretical importance. The similarities between disappearances and related phenomena involving equally serious violations of human rights can lead to confusion and inaccurate classifications. This may detract from the concept of disappearance, and so weaken the basis of humanitarian action.

Persons may be said to have disappeared in the confusion and panic following a natural disaster, or in an accident in which the body is never found. In wartime, the relatives of those on active service live in a permanent state of anxiety. They are particularly worried when they get no news. But sooner or later, news arrives, good or bad. Soldiers come home, or their families hear that they are alive, or wounded, or are prisoners of war, or are dead.

Sometimes, however, a soldier is reported as 'missing in action', when it is not known whether he has been killed in a battle or taken prisoner. As in the case of political disappearances, the family goes through prolonged agony. However, unlike the relatives of the disappeared, they can generally count on the assistance of the authorities on whose side the individual was fighting, and the details of the circumstances which resulted in a person being labelled as 'missing' are generally more accessible. Equally important, there is a well-defined system available to help families and authorities trace the whereabouts of people who are 'missing' in armed conflict situations.

Under the rule of law, even in cases where an individual has committed a loathsome crime, the accused is presumed innocent. Then, if he is found guilty and is convicted, he is punished. In both cases, before and after, his rights are clearly defined. For example, he has the right to know what he is accused of, the right to legal counsel, the right to correspond with his family, and the right to have visitors. He has a recognized legal and physical existence. His family is informed of his whereabouts and may enquire into or imagine the conditions of his imprisonment. A disappeared person, on the other hand, has no such legal status. He is struck off the register of those entitled to the protection of the law.

The key element in the definition of disappearances is the involvement of the authorities. A government is implicated in a disappearance not only by the direct participation of its officials, through the armed forces, the police, or the intelligence services, but also by the actions of unofficial groups acting with its consent, explicit or implicit. Governmental complicity often takes the form of denying all responsibility, and refusing to provide information or make enquiries.

These characteristics, which apply to most disappearances, allow us to distinguish them more clearly from other phenomena of similar kinds.

* The terms 'missing person', which is often used in the context of armed conflicts, and 'disappeared person' are sometimes treated as synonymous. The role of government, however, is not the same in both cases.

* 'Abductions', 'kidnappings', and 'taking hostages' also have many features in common with disappearances, particularly the fact that families have no way of knowing the fate of the victims. In the past, such acts were committed by individuals acting independently of governments. Today these forms of terrorism can be either 'public' or 'private'. They differ from disappearances, however, in that they are generally followed by explicit demands, e.g. for a ransom, or for some political gesture, and the fact that their perpetrators claim responsibility. In such situations, the police make enquiries and a search for the victim is undertaken. This does not occur in the case of disappearances.

* 'Detentions in conditions of secrecy' have in common with disappearances the fact that the government is implicated. In the case of the former, the individual is arrested by the police. His detention is acknowledged and his family is notified, even though visits are not permitted. In other words, the authorities do not deny their responsibility, unlike the case of disappearances. If, however, as sometimes happens, the authorities neglect or refuse to notify the prisoner's relatives, the distinction between a secret detention and a disappearance becomes very tenuous.

The same applies to persons detained in what are known as 'internment' or 'rehabilitation' camps. It often happens that the inmates are not even officially tried and convicted. Their families are not permitted to visit them, nor told when the victim will be released. Such cases cannot, however, be considered as disappearances so long as they are recognized by the authorities.

* 'Extra-judicial killings' are frequently likened to disappearances. In both cases, a political assassination takes place with the direct or indirect complicity of the authorities. Many disappearances are known to end with summary execution. In principle, however, such a practice does not constitute a disappearance unless the authorities refuse to acknowledge their responsibility and it is impossible to find out what has happened to the victim or where he is being held. No 'disappearance' has, strictly speaking, occurred

if the fate of the victim is known, if the body is found, or if the death is not kept secret.

Unlike other grave practices such as torture or genocide, no definition of 'disappearance' exists in any universally accepted document. As in all definitions of this kind, the problem arises of producing a clear, precise definition which is, at the same time, broad enough to encompass all possible cases. The issue is currently under review by the United Nations Commission on Human Rights. A draft International Convention on Enforced Disappearances has been proposed by the Latin American Federation of Associations of Relatives of Disappeared Detainees (FEDEFAM).[1] Article II states:

> For the purposes of the present Convention, the enforced disappearance of persons means any act or omission which is designed to conceal the whereabouts of a political opponent or dissident, of whose fate his family, friends or supporters are unaware, and which is committed with intent to suppress, prevent or impede opposition or dissidence, by persons in government office, by government officials at any level or by organized groups of private individuals acting with the support or permission of the foregoing.

Another definition is contained in a draft International Convention on Disappearances, submitted by the Institute of Human Rights of the Paris Bar:[2]

> The term 'enforced or involuntary disappearance' refers to all actions or events which may be detrimental to the integrity or physical or mental safety of any individual.

The first definition encompasses most of the particular features present in the practice of disappearances. It also highlights its specific nature; that is, an act of coercion in which the authorities are directly or indirectly implied. It fails, however, to take into account disappeared persons who are not political opponents. Furthermore, it makes no clear reference to the denials by authorities when faced with allegations of their involvement and their knowledge of the fate of the disappeared person.

The second definition is too broad; it makes no distinction between disappearances and violations of human rights in other similar ways.

The definition of disappearances should contain every feature characteristic of the practice: a disappearance may be said to have occurred whenever acts or omissions are committed by government agents or individuals acting with governmental consent or complicity for purposes of intimidation and repression which violate fundamental human rights, with intent to harm a person or his or her relatives, and in which public authorities conceal the fate of the victim and deny their own involvement.

Estimates of Numbers

Attempts to quantify the number of disappearances come up against the nature of the problem itself. Cases can only be recorded if they are reported to an appropriate organization, assuming, of course, that the relatives of the disappeared person are aware that such an organization exists. Even when they do know of it, they may have to overcome their fear of reprisals and must be sufficiently convincing for their information to be registered. Such an organization would then have to maintain up-to-date records and regularly publish the figures concerning new cases over a given period.

Organizations formed by the relatives of disappeared persons exist in several countries (see Chapter 3). Their principal purpose is to exert pressure at national and international levels to locate, protect and, if possible, release disappeared persons who are still alive. In carrying out this task, they must also survive the various forms of coercion and harassment to which they are almost invariably subjected and which can make their everyday lives exceedingly difficult. Operating under repressive conditions, often in semi-secrecy, it is difficult for such organizations to keep track of figures and publish regular estimates.

Nonetheless, the information which has come to light internationally has been provided by organizations of this kind, by the relatives of disappeared persons, by NGOs concerned with the protection of human rights, by religious or political groups whose activities extend to resisting the practice of disappearances, and, lastly, by individuals acting in their personal capacity.

Figures on disappearances have been published every year since 1981 by the United Nations Working Group on Enforced or Involuntary Disappearances (described in Chapter 4). The

37

methods used in compiling these figures warrant a brief description. In some of the countries where disappearances take place, there are no organizations specifically concerned with this problem, so information can only be supplied by private individuals. Furthermore, potential informants may not be aware of the existence of the Working Group. Cases not brought to its attention are those known only to a limited number of people, largely cut off from the outside world (particularly in rural areas), or those that remain concealed through ignorance of national or international organizations, or by fear of reprisals. The relatives of disappeared persons are often reluctant to transmit information in the climate of terror which the practice of disappearances produces.

The number of cases brought to the attention of the United Nations Working Group, therefore, is merely a fraction of the total. The fact that a country is not included in the Working Group's list does not necessarily mean that no disappearances occur there. The table in Chapter 4 should, therefore, be considered only as a minimum indication, both of the number of countries involved and the global number of disappearances which occur.

Published statistics only concern cases which have been brought to the attention of governments—i.e. cases substantiated by sufficient details. The figures published by the Working Group do not include information made available to the Group but which has not been analysed by the time its reports are published.

Any discrepancies between figures quoted for a given country should be no cause for surprise, therefore, since varying figures are supplied by different sources. Figures quoted by the Working Group are always lower than those obtained from other sources owing to the fact that, as indicated earlier, all disappearances are not submitted to the Working Group, the UN criteria used for substantiating cases are different to that of other organizations, and only those cases which are transmitted to governments are reported. Inevitably, the figures quoted by national and inter-governmental groups vary considerably.

In the case of Argentina, for example, while figures quoted by the press suggested that 15,000 to 30,000 persons disappeared, the Sabato Commission (the official enquiry set up by the new government) published a list of 8,960 names. During the same period the number of persons listed as disappeared by the United Nations Working Group totalled only 3,367.

Regarding Lebanon, the Committee of Relatives of Detainees, Disappeared and Abducted Persons in Lebanon estimates that the number of disappeared persons in the country is approximately 5,000. The figure of 240 quoted by the United Nations Working Group may not be an accurate reflection of the situation as data collection is impeded by the continuous armed conflict. The situation has also raised questions of overlapping responsibilities between the Working Group and the International Committee of the Red Cross. Furthermore, owing to its strictly inter-governmental mandate, the Working Group conveys the information it obtains regarding disappearances only to the Lebanese Government. It does not address the various irregular militias which claim some of the privileges of statehood and resort to abductions while denying all responsibility.

Terror and Secrecy

The question which immediately springs to mind with regard to disappearances is: why? Why does a regime make a person disappear? Why not use the normal judicial process?

Enforced disappearances are a form of deliberate terror. As a strategy, it draws its particular strength from the mystery surrounding the identity of those responsible, and from the anguish over the fate of the disappeared person which it perpetuates. The apparent irrationality involved in causing someone to disappear without allowing the family even to find out why, eliminates in practice the normal frame of reference inherent in the rule of law. Those who instigate, support and apply this method, hope that the fear it inspires will paralyse any potential opposition to the established order and increase the power of the regime they represent.

Why bother with justifications which may be disputed, or with conspicuous political trials and public executions? Why incur the condemnation of the international community? Why saddle oneself with political prisoners who arouse sympathy, or executions which fan the flames of opposition and lend it a glow of martyrdom? Arranging a disappearance is a distinctly more 'refined' solution. It is quick, and leaves no trace. It allows the authorities to claim that their hands are clean. The most effective means of terror is

39

to strike with no explanation.

In this sense, the practice of disappearances represents the acme of despotism—a form of despotism which dares not say its name and which destroys the very foundations of society. To abandon the law and the most elementary moral principles, and resort instead to underhand methods, is in itself an acknowledgement of illegitimacy.

Secrecy and disappearances are by their nature closely related. If there is no accused and no body to be found, then there can be no victim. Secrecy can be ensured by a variety of methods. In some cases, a military organization composed of several separate cells is established, where each unit is authorized to abduct individuals, to detain them in secret, and, in some cases, to execute them. In one model, individual units are co-ordinated by a central decision-making body. In other cases, the central unit itself is responsible for planning and carrying out abductions. Sometimes, the process of decision-making, planning and execution is entrusted to an irregular or paramilitary group acting on the authority of the regime.

Not only is the disappearance itself shrouded in secrecy—the same applies to the identity of its perpetrators. The employment of paramilitary groups is considered the most efficient way of handling disappearances. These groups have no legal existence, but they do have far-reaching discretionary powers which enable them to operate with impunity, outside the law, while remaining integrated within the regular security forces. They also give the authorities an alibi for claiming that political violence is the work of extremists beyond their control, thereby denying any involvement of the governmental apparatus. 'Disappearance' is the 'perfect crime'.

Recent information and analyses have brought to light some of the methods used by the agents involved and their connections with the military establishment. Such methods are usually used in cases inspired by the ideology of national security, and represent a new form of alliance between the State and the armed forces.

An ideology of this kind is based on three fundamental concepts: geopolitics, the overall strategy relating to the exercise of State authority, and the privileged role of the security apparatus and the armed forces. What matters is not the individual, but the nation, which is identified with the State. The world is the stage where the struggle for power is played out. Nations are, by definition, rivals and must fight for survival. They only exist as allies or as enemies.

This reasoning is also applied to individuals. Ultimately, no distinction is made between civilians and the military. All citizens must consider themselves in the front line, individually and collectively. Their task is to follow the national elite, namely the armed forces. The latter alone are considered appropriate trustees of the nation's destiny.

This ideology of national security dehumanizes social relations and reduces individuals to the level of objects. It breeds insecurity among citizens. It has been rightly remarked that, in this form, national security is inversely proportionate to individual security.

Under governments of this persuasion, human rights and freedoms are considered secondary to national security and are subordinated to the interests of a minority controlling both economic and military power. Typically, it is in this context that the practice of disappearances occurred in Latin America.

Besides the 36 countries listed by the UN Working Group for 1985, very little documented information is available on disappearances in other parts of the world. It would require extensive enquiries and documentary analysis of the different forms of political institutions which give rise to widespread disappearances to establish the irrefutable responsibility of governments. In general, it is difficult to see how disappearances could occur on a large scale without elaborate organization by the security apparatus. After all, decisions of this order can only be made at the highest level.

This particular form of repression is not confined to a national setting. Evidence from several different quarters suggests that it is also arranged internationally, between governments. Disappearances have occurred in the context of a deliberate, co-ordinated policy of states with converging interests and a common conception of the exercise of power. According to FEDEFAM, many Uruguayan nationals disappeared in Argentina, for example.

The governments concerned frequently accuse human rights organizations and the media of only seeing one side of the problem and failing to take so-called terrorist activities into account. It is true that in countries where disappearances occur, political tensions often run high. It is undoubtedly true, moreover, that some disappearances are perpetrated by armed groups opposing the government in power. The various militia in Lebanon, for example, bear a large share of responsibility for disappearances in that country. Governments often attribute responsibility for abductions to terrorist groups, which they use to conceal their own responsibility. A state of emergency can also be a useful alibi.

Neither war nor the fight against subversion, however, can justify contempt for the most fundamental human rights and values, which apply under all circumstances without exception, in peace and in war. (This is further discussed in Chapter 4.) Terrorism of one kind cannot justify another.

The Inter-American Commission on Human Rights made this point quite clear in the report it produced on its mission to Argentina in 1979. Violence does not solve problems; on the contrary, it exacerbates them. Acts of terrorism against the government stem from neglect of human rights, of economic and social rights, and of the need for political participation. The relationship is undoubtedly one of cause and effect.

Government in the Shadows

The practice of making opponents disappear commonly implies other violations of human rights, such as unlawful arrests, extrajudicial killings and torture. The reverse is not necessarily true. Such violations do not necessarily mean that the regime also resorts to enforced disappearances.

The practice of disappearance emerges, develops, recedes and fades away under specific conditions, which would require detailed analysis, country by country, period by period. Further research along these lines is highly desirable. Factors common to the various countries and periods in which disappearances occur could be more accurately identified. In the absence of such research, a number of observations can nonetheless be made.

In countries where human rights are seriously violated, the presence or absence of widespread disappearances does not appear to be linked so much to the apparent nature of the regime, dictatorial or democratic, as to its stability and the importance its leaders attach to the opinions of democratic countries. Not that traditional democracy is valued for its own sake. More realistically, democratic countries have a definite economic weight which must be taken into account. Unscrupulous regimes which are more or less dependent on them cannot run the risk of an open break.

South Africa is a case in point. In comparison with other countries the incidence of disappearances is relatively low. This is a reflection of the fact that the government has a sufficient arsenal of laws and regulations at its disposal to ensure the imprisonment or execution of any real or imagined opponent.

This is amply demonstrated by the events of June-July 1986 when, on the eve of the 10th anniversary of Soweto, the Pretoria regime declared a state of emergency and reinforced the tools of repression with a new range of restrictions that gives the authorities sweeping powers to deal with opponents.

South African legislation allows the authorities to detain people without any obligation to acknowledge the detention or advise the families of detainees. Even if these people are duly registered in the detention centres their families are unable to trace them and suffer similar agonies to the relatives of those who have disappeared under more clandestine circumstances.

According to the parliamentary opposition and human rights organizations in South Africa, there was no official information available to indicate where thousands of people, detained during the state of emergency, could be located. Within one month of the state of emergency proclamation, the Detainees' Parents Support Group listed more than 2,000 people, including teachers, students, trade unionists and journalists, whose whereabouts could not be established: these were described by the opposition as having 'disappeared in detention'.

At a time when the world's attention is focussed more assiduously on South Africa than ever before, the media, or whatever remains of it, has also been subjected to stringent controls in the name of state security. Foreign journalists are threatened with deportation if they publish the names of detainees, any 'unauthorized' information concerning police activities, or any other information deemed 'subversive'.

In Paraguay, despite reports of multiple human rights violations since the beginning of the present dictatorship which has already lasted 32 years, there are also relatively few disappearances. In a country such as Guatemala, on the other hand, where presidents have been constitutionally elected, disappearances have occurred on a large scale since 1966.

43

Disappeared!

The state of emergency in Paraguay has, for all intents and purposes, become a permanent feature of the political system. In its 1978 report on the human rights situation in that country, the Inter-American Commission on Human Rights noted that it was impossible to establish accurately when the state of emergency was first installed. Apart from a brief six-month interval in 1947, it seems to date back to 1929. Under these circumstances, the regime has a wide variety of means available to ensure its survival and stability. Disappearances are not, therefore, necessary. Where these do occur, however, freedom is so restricted (freedom of information and movement, for foreign journalists in particular, as well as freedom of association) that cases rarely come to light.

In Guatemala, none of the many governments, however, has succeeded in imposing its authority over the whole country. In rural areas, impoverished peasants have to struggle with great social inequalities. Opposition by them is sometimes undertaken by individuals or takes place at the purely local level. In other cases, organized opposition may range all the way from democratic trade unions to guerrilla warfare. These movements are supported by the socially aware, particularly among the urban middle class, students, the clergy, and the professions. Unlike the regime in Paraguay, however, which is indifferent to international criticism, the government of Guatemala is anxious to maintain democratic appearances, particularly in the eyes of public opinion and the United States Congress, since decisions taken there are crucially important to the Guatemalan economy.

In this context, disappearances play a double role of deterrence through terror, and repression in a form which leaves no martyrs. In theory, disappearances help maintain a façade of legality in that the authorities can feign innocence. They are nonetheless sensitive to their country's image abroad and so must also maintain a certain degree of freedom.

It is thanks to this narrow breathing space that, little by little, information circulates; proof of the authorities' responsibility can be documented, and associations of the relatives of disappeared persons can be formed. International opinion is therefore gradually being made aware, and the crime is no longer entirely secret.

Disappearances may persist, however, because of their convenience to weak regimes, which consider it in their interest to arrest without proof and execute without process of law. This approach is all the more likely when the reaction by the international community is inadequate.

This explains the large numbers of disappearances which occurred in Chile during the months following the military coup in September 1973, as one element in the widespread political repression. Peasants from central Chile and government officials belonging to the Unidad Popular party alike were arrested by the armed forces without a warrant. They were then executed or died under torture. The authorities claimed total ignorance about their fate. In June 1974, the creation of DINA (the National Intelligence Directorate) under the direct authority of the Head of the Junta allowed disappearances to be planned more carefully and carried out more discreetly, using agents in plain clothes, in special detention centres, and with no witnesses. As the Junta became more securely established, a new arsenal of laws was drawn up which placed increasing restrictions on the exercise of civil liberties.

During this period, international opinion was losing interest in repression in the country, and the leader of the Junta, aware of fading international protests, was able to consolidate his power. In these conditions, a strong dictatorship no longer needed to resort to disappearances on a large scale as an element of policy.

The practice of enforced disappearances frequently appears in the context of a state of emergency declared either throughout the whole country or, as in some cases of guerrilla warfare, in a particular area. As noted above, Paraguay is an isolated case since the state of emergency in that country has become permanent apparently without provoking mass disappearances.

It is worth recalling that a state of emergency implies the concentration of political power in a single arm of government—the executive. Special powers are granted to the Head of State or the ruling junta at the expense of the Parliament, which is either abolished or largely stripped of its power. Laws are made by decree, on the strength of executive authority alone. The jurisdiction of special courts, usually military, is extended to include civilian cases. This may entail summary procedures, the violation or reduction of the rights of the defence, the application or extension of capital punishment, the granting of special powers to the police, and press censorship.

It is true that a state of emergency and the suspension of certain safeguards are legitimate in the eyes of national constitutions and international law. It is equally true, however, that such measures must be temporary and be subject to certain controls. What is reprehensible is the abuse of such procedures; for example, when they are used as a pretext to eliminate political opponents and to reduce or restrict the responsibility of public authorities.

There are also other anomalies. Sometimes, for example, the state of emergency comes into being without ever being formally declared, or may be similarly lifted. As noted above, the state of emergency may become permanent, so that the exception becomes the rule.

Certain countries resort to more subtle forms of a state of emergency; these are sometimes called 'restricted' democracies. This gives the regime a veneer of legitimacy and institutionalizes the role of the army in political life. In some constitutions, this temporary state of affairs may be prolonged over a period of several years, during which the armed forces keep ultimate control over the political process.

These different forms of abuse reveal the clear need for more effective international monitoring of states of emergency. Here again, the legality of such situations is not at issue. What matters is the risk of overstepping the law, and the violations of human rights which this may generate. If countries in a state of emergency were 'kept under observation', certain violations of human rights, including disappearances, might be prevented.

There is no need for regimes which consistently violate human rights and which are impervious to international opinion to resort systematically to disappearances. In the impenetrable obscurity of a well-established dictatorship, disappearances serve no purpose. Legal pitfalls, in ample number, are already strewn on either side of the path to reduce those who stray to silence. In democracies, too, authorities may sometimes be tempted to by-pass human rights, especially when they face a crisis or are confronted with violence. But in an open society, in the light of public scrutiny, the risks in doing so are greater and the balance of power comes into play. Disappearances are essentially the deeds of insecure dictatorships or semi-democracies, both of which are dependent on outside support, and which have reason to fear public opinion in countries whose support they need.

Disappearances are a product of shadowy, twilight regimes—regimes which sink into unrelenting tyranny or, on the contrary, are painfully clawing their way towards better days, without having the required means to do so. They occur in countries with traditions of democratic government which resist the imposition of dictatorship, as in Argentina, or in those burdened with a dictatorial heritage which can paralyse the process of reform, as in Guatemala and El Salvador.

For such regimes, international public opinion plays an important role, not only because they are sensitive about their image, but also because public opinion can demand that all external aid be contingent on a real improvement in civil liberties and a more equitable distribution of economic and social benefits.

Notes

1. E/CN.4/1985/15, Annex III, p. 1.
2. *Le refus de l'oubli: Paris Colloquium, Janvier- Février 1981*, Berger-Levrault, Paris, 1982, p. 314.

3. Disappearances, Human Rights and International Ethics

Wherever law ends, tyranny begins.

John Locke, 1690

Rights Trampled

Unlike genocide and torture, no specific provision for disappearances has been made in international legal instruments relating to human rights. It represents, nonetheless, a serious breach of the fundamental principles of human rights which are universally recognized. Disappearances infringe an entire range of human rights, particularly:

* The right to life: disappeared persons may be arbitrarily executed or may die in detention through cruel treatment or from lack of care.
* The right to liberty and security of the person, as well as other rights which derive from it, such as the right not to be subjected to arbitrary arrest, the right to a fair trial, and the right to recognition as a person before the law.
* The right to humane conditions of detention, and the right not to be subjected to torture or to cruel, inhuman or degrading treatment or punishment.

These rights are enshrined in the Universal Declaration of Human Rights.[1] Similar provisions are made by legal instruments such as the International Covenant on Civil and Political Rights, the American Convention on Human Rights, the European Convention on Human Rights, the African Charter of Human Rights and Peoples, and the Geneva Conventions of 1949 and their Additional Protocols of 1977.

Disappeared!

The practice of disappearances also constitutes a breach of other instruments adopted by the United Nations, namely the Declaration on the Protection of all Persons from being Subjected to Torture and other Cruel, Inhuman or Degrading Treatment or Punishment, the Principles of Medical Ethics, the Code of Conduct for Law Enforcement Officials, as well as the Standard Minimum Rules for the Treatment of Prisoners. These rules are applicable to all types of detainees, criminal or civil, before or after conviction, including those detained for security reasons. The rules require that the following provisions in particular be respected:

* A bound register must be maintained, showing for each detainee the reasons for detention, the competent authority decreeing the detention, and the date and time of admission and release;
* Prisoners must be allowed to communicate with their families;
* In case of death or serious illness, the authorities must inform the detainee's spouse or next of kin; prisoners have the right to inform their family immediately of their detention or of their transfer to another establishment;
* Prisoners placed on remand also have the right to inform their families of their detention immediately.[2]

No provision stipulates that these rules apply to political prisoners. Nevertheless, they were considered by the United Nations Congress on the Prevention of Crime and the Treatment of Offenders (Kyoto, 1970) as being equally applicable to this category of detainee.

As indicated above, the practice of disappearances also affects women (including pregnant women) and children. In this context, several specific rights are affected, namely:

* Rights intended to ensure the care of children, pregnant women and nursing mothers.[3] These rights are linked to the protection of the right to life, which is protected by the American Convention on Human Rights from the moment of conception (Article 4).
* The right of every child to a personal identity. By virtue of this right, children born in detention centres should be registered immediately after their birth and should have a name.[4]
* The right of every child to the care and protection of his

parents. The Declaration on the Rights of the Child proclaimed by the United Nations in 1959 provides that the child shall grow up in the care and under the responsibility of his parents, and that a small child shall not be separated from his or her mother.

The practice of disappearances infringes the right to a family life, as well as several rights of an economic, social and cultural nature (the right to an adequate standard of living, and the right to the education of the family, for example). The family is the natural and fundamental unit of society and is entitled to protection by society and the State.[5]

In the case of armed conflicts, the Geneva Conventions of 1949 and their Additional Protocols of 1977 contain provisions concerning the protection of the family unit and the right of the child not to be separated from the family even in the case of detention, as well as the right of families to reunification. These instruments proclaim the basic principle to be followed in cases of disappearance, namely, 'the right of families to know the fate of their members'.[6] This principle is reaffirmed by resolutions of the United Nations and the International Red Cross.

The right to life, the right not to be subjected to torture or to cruel, inhuman or degrading treatment, and the right to recognition as a person before the law are all inalienable rights. The fact that they apply even under states of emergency underscores the considerable legal value accorded to them.

The Charter of the United Nations and the Universal Declaration of Human Rights are universally recognized. They are binding on all states. The Universal Declaration proclaims the rights, duties and moral values on which a consensus exists, even if practice falls far short of theory. This consensus was expressed by the International Conference on Human Rights at Teheran in 1968, which proclaimed that 'The Universal Declaration of Human Rights states an understanding common to the peoples of the world concerning the inalienable and inviolable rights of all members of the human family and constitutes an obligation for the members of the international community'.

The Declaration defines the highest aspiration of humankind, namely, 'the advent of a world in which human beings shall enjoy freedom of speech and belief, freedom from fear and want ...' According to the Preamble to the Declaration, this universal

51

aspiration should be 'an ideal common to all peoples and all nations'. By this criterion, the 'conscience of mankind' must condemn all practices which are contrary to human dignity. By the same standard, the General Assembly of the Organization of American States declared in 1983 that the practice of disappearances was an affront to the conscience of the continent and a crime against mankind.

Indeed, the practice of disappearances is degrading not only for the victim but also for the government concerned, which uses terror as the foundation of its power. Power of this kind strays from its proper objectives and forfeits its moral and political justification. Society in its entirety is debased when some of its members persecute their fellow men, and hold the most elementary civic and humanitarian principles in contempt.

Justice Fettered

The reactions of a disappeared person's relatives frequently go through several different stages. The first is one of paralysis for fear of reprisals, not only against themselves but also against the victim they hope is still alive. They conceal what they know, even among members of the family. Asking too many questions, they feel, may precipitate the victim's death.

It is important to remember that in many countries the family, friends and lawyers of the victim are not automatically informed after an arrest has been made. Silence and inactivity make relatives feel guilty, and prompt them to start searching. The first step is to contact local police stations and detention centres. Sometimes they can obtain the help of a senior official they may know in the government hierarchy. Generally, however, the authorities will deny all knowledge or simply refuse to answer requests for information.

Discretionary powers to dispense with certain procedures such as legally informing the family in case of arrest create conditions favourable to disappearances, secret detentions, extra-judicial killings and torture. Discretionary powers of this kind are often provided for in the laws governing states of emergency or in martial law, and allow, notably, for secret detention over long periods.

In South Africa, for example, the Internal Security Act specifically authorizes the authorities not to inform relatives of the detention of a family member.

Having realized the futility of making enquiries at local police stations, and that pursuing this course of action would be both useless and dangerous, the relatives of disappeared persons turn to legal channels. The principal recourse within a given country is through the courts, where the relatives can request a writ of habeas corpus or *amparo*, or similar procedures.

The procedure known as habeas corpus, which literally means 'you should have your body', was introduced into English law in the 17th century. It exists also in the common law of many other countries, particularly in Latin America, where it is sometimes known as *amparo*. This term, first used in Mexico in the 19th century, means 'protection'. In general, its application is somewhat wider than that of habeas corpus. Minor details apart, however, the object of both these procedures is identical, namely to ensure an enquiry into cases of detention which fail to comply with the methods prescribed by law. The official responsible is summoned to appear before the court to explain the reasons for the detention and to produce the detainee. If incarceration is found to be unjustified, the court orders the immediate release of the prisoner.

The essence of these procedures is included in the International Covenant on Civil and Political Rights (Article 9), according to which 'Anyone deprived of his liberty by arrest or detention shall be entitled to the right of appeal before a court, which will pronounce without delay on the legality of his detention and order his release if it is found not to be lawful.'

The many limitations placed on this right of appeal, however, may tend to nullify it in practice. Recourse procedures, for example, are frequently not allowed when the prisoner is detained for political or national security reasons, and may be suspended if a state of emergency is declared.

In the Philippines, before the recent change in regime, habeas corpus was suspended in two regions of Mindanao Island, even though martial law had been lifted in January 1981 (Proclamation No. 2045 by President Ferdinand Marcos). Furthermore, persons detained for alleged crimes of subversion or armed insurrection anywhere in the Philippines had no right of habeas corpus.

In some countries, the regime maintains the trappings of habeas corpus or *amparo* and other basic institutions of a democratic state, but indirectly and subtly manages to block their application in practice. One such tactic consists of the organized or forced complicity or passivity of the judiciary, which then becomes no more than a tool to rubber-stamp blatantly illegal practices. In Chile, for example, the government can obtain a certificate stating the presumed death of a disappeared person. Once this document has been issued, the victim's relatives may no longer file a request for habeas corpus or take legal action.

There is naturally no chance of an appeal succeeding if there is no guarantee that magistrates and lawyers can act independently. In 1977, the International Commission of Jurists [7], reporting on Uganda, found that all efforts by the courts to respect legal procedures were foiled by the interference of the military.

Magistrates and lawyers who have the courage of their convictions are often pressurized by the authorities. In El Salvador, for example, several magistrates have been threatened, executed or abducted, for doing no more than their duty. In Uganda, impartial or independent judgments were punished by abduction and disappearance.[8]

According to a 1976 report on the Philippines by Amnesty International,[9] judges showing independence of mind were deemed to be undesirable and relieved of their duties. In 1980, changes in the legal system undermined the role of judges and encroached on their independence.[10] It is hoped that the new government in the Philippines will restore the integrity, independence and credibility of the judiciary.

After sending a mission to Argentina in 1979, the New York Bar Association, in its report, underscored the powerlessness, or bad faith, of the courts.[11] According to its information, requests for habeas corpus were automatically rejected once the authorities denied having any information on the disappeared person. Over 10,000 requests for habeas corpus were rejected in this way. According to the Grandmothers of the Plaza de Mayo, the total number of requests for habeas corpus in Argentina amounted to 100,000.

In Chile, several requests were rejected despite clear proof of the victims' arrest. Of the 5,000 requests filed for *amparo* only four were admitted.[12]

The effectiveness of the legal apparatus is a prerequisite in the struggle against disappearances. Habeas corpus and *amparo* provide concrete lifelines for the relatives of disappeared persons. In those countries where no similar procedures exist, clear legislation on detention must be established.

In reaction to the rise of fascism in the 1930s, it was suggested that an international writ of habeas corpus should be created with international courts. The purpose was to empower these to act on appeals for habeas corpus once all national channels had been exhausted or where no safeguards of independent legal proceedings applied.

This suggestion, which was revived in a resolution by the United Nations Sub-Commission on the Prevention of Discrimination and Protection of Minorities (5.B XXXII, 5-9-79), was never implemented. It conflicts with the concept states have of their national sovereignty. Legal bodies established on a regional basis, such as the Inter-American Court of Human Rights, do exist, however, and it would be perfectly conceivable to establish courts with regional competence for cases of habeas corpus and *amparo*.

Words Suppressed

Under a dictatorship where human rights are held in contempt, the media are closely controlled. Their power is enormous, as they are potentially in a strong position to denounce the practices of the regime and to reveal unacceptable facts to the public. Thousands of human lives may depend on their attitude.

When a dictatorial regime comes to power, the press is frequently divided into two camps, at least initially. One camp sides with the government and becomes its accomplice, either by keeping silent or by openly supporting its theory and practice. The other resists and denounces it. The former thrives on 'night and fog', the latter aim to bring the truth into the light of day. In Chile, for example, the press did not mention the phenomenon of disappearances until the Association of Relatives of Disappeared Persons organized a hunger strike in 1977. Until then, the press had only spoken in terms of 'accusations, fabrications, and political tricks designed to discredit the government'. Newspapers went so far as to publish false reports, including articles which specifically stated that reported disappearances had not occurred. The Special Rapporteur appointed by the United Nations to enquire into the fate of disappeared persons in Chile declared in this context that: 'The failure of the Chilean mass media to report the facts was certainly a factor which contributed to the continuation of disappearances.'[13]

Journalists courageous enough to fulfil their function of providing information run the risk of censorship and reprisals. Many have been threatened, killed or have themselves been abducted for trying to investigate and report on violations of human rights in their country. In Argentina nearly 70 journalists were victim of this fate. In South Africa, for example, one month after the proclamation of the state of emergency in June 1986, the Detainees' Parents Support Committee reported the detention of twelve journalists.

In November 1984, the Guatemalan Association of Democratic Journalists submitted a petition to the National Assembly, requesting it to intervene on behalf of 22 journalists who had disappeared, and to explain clearly how 23 others had been assassinated. The Association claimed to have direct or indirect proof of the involvement of the security forces in the murders.

Where the national press is subject to censorship, the public can count only on the international media. National associations formed by the relatives of disappeared persons then have a vital role in passing on information.

Foreign correspondents can, of course, be prevented from investigating and reporting on certain subjects for fear of expulsion. They are often not authorized to circulate freely, or even to enter the country. The act of reporting regardless of the consequences, and of breaking through the walls of silence, is hazardous indeed, and fraught with the risk of reprisals.

Organized Resistance

When individual action is ineffective and the courts fail to provide legal protection, a common reaction is the formation of associations often spearheaded by the relatives of the disappeared. Medical evidence suggests that the mutual support such associations generate among the relatives of disappeared persons serves an important therapeutic purpose.

'When I saw all those people who had got together', said one mother whose son had disappeared, 'I began to understand that I was not alone in my sadness, and that hundreds, or even thousands, of other mothers were feeling the same pain. Those who have not been through it can't know what it's like. People say ''I'm sorry, I am very sad for you, I understand.'' But nothing has happened to them. It's only words. Here in our association we understand one another because we have all been through it. We have all felt the same pain.'

The overall objective of these associations is to attract the attention of the general public and exert pressure on the government. The hunger strikes by the Chilean Association of Relatives of Disappeared Persons, the demonstrations organized by the Grandmothers of the Plaza de Mayo in central Buenos Aires and by Lebanese and Palestinian women in Beirut, have all alerted the press and public opinion, and contributed significantly to exposing the problem of disappearances.

Owing to the harassment and reprisals to which the relatives of disappeared persons are exposed, creating such associations requires a great deal of courage. Searching for those who are missing is sometimes seen as a subversive act, and support groups are often labelled accomplices of 'communist' organizations.

In Guatemala, for example, the Mutual Support Group for the Return of Missing Relatives Alive (GAM) was formed in June 1984, with the support of the Rector of the University of San Carlos and the Guatemalan Conference of Religious Congregations (CONFREGUA). After staging several public demonstrations, such as a march by several hundred people to the cathedral, and the peaceful organization of an inaugural General Assembly, representatives of GAM were received by the President of Guatemala on 1 August 1984, and again on 19 and 20 November. Despite this official recognition, however, several members received death threats and pressure was exerted on the press to refuse public notices paid for by GAM. On 30 March 1985, the spokesman for the group was abducted. His mutilated body was found on a roadside the following day. The Vice-President of GAM, whose husband had disappeared in May 1984, was kidnapped on 4 April 1985. She was killed along with her brother and two-year-old son. Her husband had been the son of the founding President of the Guatemalan Commission on Human Rights and a former Rector of the University of San Carlos.

The fact that those responsible for disappearances also hound the relatives of disappeared persons who form associations is proof

57

that the latter can have a major impact and have a very important role to play. They provide moral support and practical help to relatives, seek out information on individual cases, and approach the authorities, courts and international organizations on behalf of the families concerned.

The activities of such organizations are also an important lifeline to the people who have been abducted. The knowledge that others are concerned about their fate undoubtedly provides some comfort, however intangible. Although there is no means of communication, news sometimes filters through. Those who disappear after the creation of a support organization, for example, are often instrumental in passing word along. These associations also serve to sharpen national and international public awareness of the problem. Many have offices abroad. In Latin America, several associations are affiliated, or may co-ordinate their activities at the regional level. The Latin American Federation of Associations of Relatives of Disappeared Detainees (FEDEFAM), and the Central American Association of Relatives of Disappeared Persons, are two such examples.

There are many concrete examples which attest to the effectiveness of these associations and the importance of international support. The Chilean association, Protection of Children Affected by the State of Emergency (PIDEE), funded by foreign aid, owns its own premises, and is staffed by a team of psychologists, sociologists and doctors who help the children of the disappeared.

Thanks to their knowledge of the local situation and the information made available to them, these non-governmental organizations (NGOs) also form a vital link with international bodies opposed to the practice of disappearances. Task Force of the Philippines (TFOP), for example, has a thorough, well-organized documentation and research programme. It regularly publishes reports of its activities and sends copies to international organizations, particularly the United Nations Working Group on Enforced and Involuntary Disappearances, and to Amnesty International.

The practice of establishing NGOs in this field is far more developed in Latin America than in other parts of the world. This is evidenced by the list of organizations with which the United Nations Working Group is in contact.[14] It is partly due to the sophistication of urban development in the area and the lasting achievements of intermittent periods of democracy; Latin American countries have long been known to alternate between the joy of free elections and the sorrow of repression.

The lack of NGOs and local human rights organizations in other parts of the world, together with poor communication networks, explains why disappearances outside Latin America have attracted so little attention. There is scant information, for example, about the number of disappearances in many countries in Asia, the Middle East and elsewhere. The experience of Latin American NGOs, both in their strategy and their tactics, must serve as a source of inspiration for taking up the struggle in other countries.

Notes

1. Articles 3,5,6,9,10,11.
2. Rules 7, 37, 44, 92.
3. Articles 25 of the Universal Declaration of Human Rights; 24 of the International Covenant on Civil and Political Rights; 10 of the International Covenant on Economic, Social and Cultural Rights; 19 of the American Convention on Human Rights; the Declaration on the Rights of the Child.
4. Articles 24 of the International Covenant on Civil and Political Rights; 24, 50 and 136 of the Fourth Geneva Convention; and 78 of Additional Protocol I.
5. Articles 23 of the International Covenant on Civil and Political Rights; 17 of the American Convention; and 18 of the African Charter of Human Rights and Peoples.
6. Article 32 of Protocol I.
7. *Uganda and Human Rights: Report to the United Nations Commission on Human Rights*, ICJ, 1977.
8. *'Disappearances': A Workbook*. An Amnesty International (USA) Publication, 1981, pp. 158-159.
9. *Report of an Amnesty International Mission to the Republic of the Philippines*, AI, 1976.
10. See *The Philippines: Human Rights after Martial Law*, ICJ, 1984.
11. *Report of the Mission of Lawyers to Argentina*, 1-7 April 1979, p. 14.
12. Amnesty International, SF.84 CA 310-ACT.03/02/84, p. 4.
13. A/34/583/add.1, 21 November 1979, p. 74.
14. E/CN.4/1985/15, p. 8.

4. The Role of Inter-Governmental Organizations

Much of what is done will one day prove to have been of little avail. That is no excuse for the failure to act in accordance with our best understanding, in recognition of its limits but with faith in the ultimate result of the creative evolution in which it is our privilege to co-operate.

Dag Hammarskjöld

The scale of the problem of disappearances and the shortcomings of national means of redress have prompted several international, governmental and non-governmental organizations to take steps to help combat the phenomenon.

In this respect, the United Nations Working Group on Enforced or Involuntary Disappearances, which was established with the specific purpose of dealing with the problem, plays a relatively active role.

The United Nations Working Group on Enforced or Involuntary Disappearances

Concern by the United Nations over disappearances was initially limited to only two countries: Cyprus and Chile. It was not until 1978 that the General Assembly first recognized the practice of disappearances as a widespread problem, and expressed deep concern about 'reports from various parts of the world relating to enforced or involuntary disappearance of persons as a result of excesses on the part of law enforcement or security authorities'.[1]

On the same occasion, the General Assembly requested the United Nations Commission on Human Rights to examine the issue and to make appropriate recommendations. In 1980, the Commission created the Working Group on Enforced or Involuntary Disappearances. The Group consists of five members of the Commission, who act in their personal capacity. Its establishment was the first specific step taken at the inter-governmental level in response to the problem.

The method of work adopted by the Group is relatively well adapted to its objectives and the means available to it. It primarily entails immediate intervention through direct person-to-person contact, while enlisting the co-operation of the government concerned. Because each individual case requires a quick reaction, the Working Group has adopted procedures unprecedented within the United Nations. Immediately after learning of an abduction, the Chairman of the Group is authorized to send a cable to the government concerned asking for clarification. This procedure is frequently used. It enables the Group to be constantly at the disposal of the families affected and to act swiftly to save human lives. In the opinion of the Working Group, this procedure may also have had a preventive influence over other potential cases.

Since its creation in 1980, the emergency procedure for contacting governments has been used by the Group in 1,121 cases. 195 such messages were transmitted in 1984.[2]

One of the most striking characteristics of the reports published by the Group is the difference between the number of cases submitted to governments and the number of cases resolved (see table). Governments show very little inclination to co-operate, and the Group has practically no means of exerting pressure on them to do so. Replies received are often dilatory. One standard reply consists of stating that the persons concerned disappeared during clashes between opposing factions. Another standard response is the claim that the person has left the country, or is a common criminal, or has disappeared for personal reasons. Other replies are equally evasive. The former government of Argentina, for example, without giving any concrete explanation about the cases of disappearance submitted to it by the Group, claimed that they were trumped-up fabrications and were part of an overall campaign intended to discredit it. Similarly, the government of Ethiopia contested the Group's information and claimed that its sources were trying to

Disappearance Cases and Government Responses, 1985

COUNTRY	Total no. of cases transmitted to governments by the Working Group	Total no. of government responses	Cases clarified by government responses	Cases clarified by non-governmental sources
Argentina	3,393	845	31	17
Brazil	44	9	0	0
Cyprus	Since 1980, the Group has transmitted 2,400 disappearance cases to the Governments of Turkey and Cyprus. The Group provides assistance to the Committee on Missing Persons in Cyprus, which resumed its activities in 1984.			
Colombia	183	21	10	0
El Salvador	2,296	352	279	12
Guatemala	2,156	39	19	20
Honduras	123	73	12	12
Indonesia	76	0	0	2
Iran	58	0	0	0
Iraq	111	56	10	0
Lebanon	240	0	0	0
Nicaragua	199	157	38	21
Peru	872	76	21	20
Philippines	443	245	70	3
Sri Lanka	197	9	3	0
Uruguay	53	24	6	0

Notes:
1. In some cases, these figures include disappearances which occurred in previous years.
2. Countries in which less than 20 disappearances occurred are not included in the Table.
3. The Working Group has not dealt with disappearances in Chile that occurred before its creation, in view of the mandate of the UN Special Rapporteur on Chile. Between 1973 and 1985, human rights groups reported 700 disappearances.

Source: Report of the Working Group E/CN/4/1986/18, 24th January 1986.

slander the country. Indonesia conceded that each individual case was indeed an important matter but that the government had nonetheless decided to allocate its limited resources to other needs. Reactions such as these have prompted certain organizations to suggest that, in cases where governments refuse to co-operate, their replies should be handed over to the UN Human Rights Commission and made public.

In addition to the lack of co-operation by governments and its inability to exert any pressure, the effectiveness of the Working Group is restricted by other factors, namely:

* The Group only investigates cases which have been brought to its attention by others; it does not actively seek out information and does not publicize its existence in the countries concerned. Admittedly, two of its recent sessions were held in places other than the UN offices in Geneva or New York (one was held in San José, Costa Rica, in 1984, and the other in Buenos Aires in 1985), and two members of the Group were invited to carry out a mission to Peru in June 1985. Although external meetings such as these can give the Group some useful publicity and enable it to meet the families and NGOs directly concerned, such meetings cannot take place without the authorization and collaboration of the government concerned. The meeting in Buenos Aires, for example, was held at the invitation of the new civilian government of Argentina.

* Because cases are known to have occurred more frequently in Latin America than elsewhere, the Working Group is sometimes accused of geographical bias. In reality, this situation is partly due, as mentioned above, to the existence and effectiveness of Latin American NGOs.

* Like other organizations, the work of the Group is hampered by a degree of bureaucracy and the constraints inherent in its procedures. Before a case can be officially recognized, for example, it must fulfil certain conditions. Requirements such as the full name of the victim, date of birth, the place where the abduction occurred, reports by witnesses, etc. are not always included in communications received by the Group. Similarly, information is sometimes submitted to the Group by NGOs which fails to comply with the required format and so cannot even be recorded.

* There is a certain discrepancy between the size and the resources of the Group and its work-load. In 1985, for example, it received

information on 4,500 cases, but barely managed to submit 50% of them to governments. The growing number of unsatisfactory and contradictory replies received from governments frequently requires careful and time-consuming investigation.

In other words, the Group can scarcely be expected to work miracles. Indeed, in one of its reports the Group itself recognized that the problem was too vast and complex for it to deal with adequately, or even to process all the communications it received properly.[3]

There is undoubtedly an urgent need for improvement. This point is discussed in greater detail in Chapter 6.

The Human Rights Committee

The Human Rights Committee was established in the context of the International Covenant on Civil and Political Rights. It was established in 1976 when the Covenant entered into force, and consists of 18 experts who serve in their personal capacity. Although no provision is made for official relations between the Committee and non-governmental organizations, it frequently receives information from them. The Committee's role consists of making reports and considering complaints filed by States or individuals, to ensure that the States Parties to the Covenant fulfil their obligations under it. To carry out its task, the Committee can use three types of procedures:

* Under Article 40, the Committee considers reports submitted by States Parties to the Covenant on the measures they have adopted to implement its provisions. These reports are examined in public and in the presence of a representative of the State concerned, who may be questioned. The Committee may address its general observations directly to governments.

* Under Article 41, the Committee may consider communications formulated by a State relating to another State. Such communications may only be considered by the Committee if the States concerned have formally recognized the competence of the Committee. This procedure enables a State which considers that another State has failed to live up to its obligations under the Covenant to

refer the matter to the Committee.

* The Committee may receive and consider communications submitted by individuals, provided that they are within the jurisdiction of a State which has ratified the Optional Protocol to the Covenant. This procedure allows individuals claiming to be victims of violations of any of the rights set out in the Covenant, or third parties acting on their behalf, to submit communications to the Committee on Human Rights.

The procedure established by the Covenant is, however, subject to certain limitations, namely:

* Communications considered by the Committee only result in 'observations' or 'findings'. The only way the Committee can pass 'judgement' on a State which fails to fulfil its obligations is to publish an account of the case in its annual report to the General Assembly of the United Nations.

* By 1984, only 80 States had acceded to the Covenant on Civil and Political Rights. This is still an insufficient number.

* Only 17 States have signed the declaration provided for by Article 41 recognizing the competence of the Committee to receive communications made by States concerning other States, and only 34 are parties to the Optional Protocol granting the Committee the right to consider communications from individuals.

* Procedures are slow and inappropriate to the urgent situations created by disappearances. This is a typical feature of most procedures established by conventions of this kind, such as the Convention against Torture, and regional conventions on human rights.

The publication of reports does, however, have a deterrent effect, since governments are often more sensitive to public criticism than one may believe.

The 'findings' of the Human Rights Committee help to define the general rules of conduct for all States, even those which are not Parties to the Covenant or which do not accept the monitoring measures provided for. In certain circumstances the Committee is also empowered to give its opinion on concepts which are frequently invoked by governments to justify their actions, such as 'national security', 'law and order', 'state of war', etc.

Lastly, the Committee could play an important role in preventing disappearances by means of its monitoring of the establishment and implementation of states of emergency, as provided for by Article 4 of the Covenant. Article 4 imposes restrictions on States, in particular that of never being able to derogate from absolute rights, the same rights which are specifically affected by the practice of disappearances, namely the right to life, to protection from torture and other cruel, inhuman or degrading treatment, and the right to recognition as a person before the law.

During the consideration of one case (Consuelo Salgar de Montejo, Colombia), the Committee declared that:

> Although the substantive right to take derogative measures may not depend on a formal notification being made pursuant to Article 4, Paragraph 3 of the Covenant, the State party concerned is duty bound, when it invokes Article 4, Paragraph 1 of the Covenant in proceedings under the Optional Protocol to give a sufficiently detailed account of the relevant facts to show that a situation of the kind described in Article 4, Paragraph 1 of the Covenant exists in the country concerned.[4]

International Labour Organization (ILO)

The ILO, a specialized agency of the United Nations system, has adopted numerous conventions relating to human rights such as freedom of association, protection from forced labour, and non-discrimination. Various procedures exist which enable the ILO to follow up and monitor the application of these conventions. Although none of the instruments applied by the ILO directly concerns disappearances, it is obliged to deal with the problem when trade unionists and the right to participate in trade union activity are affected.

Several complaints regarding the disappearance of trade unionists have been received by the Committee on Freedom of Association, which is empowered to consider complaints from unions, employers' organizations and governments, even if the government concerned has not ratified the conventions relating to freedom of association. Several means of intervention are available to the ILO which enable it to respond to emergency situations. In cases where governments fail to provide a satisfactory response, for example, the Director-

Disappeared!

General may request additional information directly from the authorities concerned without waiting for the next meeting of the Committee.

The Director-General can also have recourse to an emergency procedure by which a case is given priority on the agenda. Provided the Chairman of the Committee agrees, the Director-General may also resort to the 'direct contact' procedure, which consists of sending a representative to the country concerned. This procedure was used in 1978, in particular with regard to the disappearance of trade union leaders in Argentina. Although the persons in question were never found, the procedure at least made it possible to bring pressure to bear on the government.

United Nations Educational, Scientific, and Cultural Organization (UNESCO)

UNESCO's activities encompass rights concerning education, science, culture and communication, including the right to liberty of opinion and expression. It has established a procedure by which complaints may be filed by individuals, and by NGOs, (national or international), having reliable information on human rights violations in these areas.

With regard to disappearances of teachers, for example, the Committee on Conventions and Recommendations may apply a special procedure. This form of investigation was adopted in 1978, and is equally applicable in cases of collective, flagrant and systematic violations as it is in individual cases.

During the course of its meetings, which are held in the presence of representatives of the government concerned, the Committee may hear evidence from witnesses or from the author of the communication. The Committee may also decide to request the Director-General to use his good offices to deal with the cases brought to its attention.

The deterrent which the Committee may use is publication of complaints in its report. It may also submit cases of human rights violations to the General Conference of UNESCO. Since the Committee only receives one hundred or so complaints per year, however, its activities do not appear to be widely known.

European Institutions

For over 40 years, European institutions have established organizations and developed legal instruments appropriate to the defence of human rights in Europe, as well as outside it. This corpus of jurisprudence, precedent, and parliamentary practice encompasses the whole spectrum of human rights.

Since their foundation, the Council of Europe and the European Economic Community have felt particularly well-placed to act in this field. They were sustained in their efforts by the determination of their member countries to reaffirm their attachment to democracy and to unite their efforts to safeguard freedom and the rights of the individual.

Membership of these organizations is indeed subject to respect for democratic principles and practice, as the statutes of the Council of Europe and the Treaty of Rome specifically state. Regarding human rights, they have a triple function:

* In legislation, the Council of Europe prepares conventions which are submitted for signature and ratification to Member States;
* In Community law, which applies to Member States, whether it is directly applicable or not;
* In the political action of parliamentary institutions.

The Council of Europe

To 'safeguard and develop human rights' is one of the main objectives of the Council of Europe. The European Convention on Human Rights was signed in 1950. It came into force in 1953 and is binding on the 21 Member States of the Council of Europe. Its monitoring mechanism operates on both legal and political levels.

Jurisdictional control is undertaken by the European Commission of Human Rights and the European Court of Human Rights. Any State Party to the Convention may bring an alleged violation before the Commission and invoke a breach of the Convention by another State Party (Article 24).

The exceptional nature of the Convention lies not only in the commitment of its States, on the basis of their ratification, to the pursuit of human rights, but also in the recognition of private individuals as legal persons in their own right. Any individual who feels that his or her rights have been infringed may seek redress from the government he or she considers responsible. Such a procedure can be rightly considered revolutionary in comparison with the interpretation hitherto given to this right. For the first time, a forum exists where a private citizen has the possibility of sueing the government on the basis of international law. In a way, it represents a substantive derogation of the State's authority. The right of individual recourse is conditional, however, on specific adherence to this provision on the part of States. To date, four member States— Greece, Liechtenstein, Malta and Turkey—have not yet declared their acceptance.

Although the European Court has exercised its jurisdiction on relatively rare occasions since its creation, its role is no less significant as its judgements deal with issues closely related to basic freedom, such as telephone tapping, the freedom of the press, certain forms of statutory detention, etc.

The monitoring mechanisms of the Council of Europe have to date not been called upon to deal with any case of disappearance requested by a private citizen. The European Commission on Human Rights, however, has investigated the fate of persons who disappeared in Cyprus (Case of Cyprus v. Turkey). It sent a mission to carry out on-the-spot enquiries, and reported on the difficulties encountered in certifying cases and establishing facts due to lack of access to the northern part of the island and to Turkish detention centres. The Commission felt nonetheless that it had sufficient evidence to conclude that Turkey had violated certain provisions of the Convention, which it had signed and ratified.

It is worth noting, however, that Turkey has signed, but not ratified, certain other provisions relating to the individual right of recourse to the Commission on Human Rights, and on the binding character of the Court's jurisdiction.

Although European countries themselves are only marginally concerned with the problem of disappearances, the Council of Europe adopted a Recommendation on the subject in 1979. It urges States to cooperate in the search for disappeared persons and in exchanging information. Each State is called upon to designate a national body to act as a reference centre for all matters relating to the subject. In 1984, moreover, the Parliamentary Assembly of the Council of Europe adopted a resolution condemning the practice of disappearances as a 'crime against humanity'.

Political monitoring of the Convention is the responsibility of the Committee of Ministers of the Council of Europe. The Committee is called upon to act as a monitoring body for the Convention in cases which are not brought before the Court. If it finds that a violation of the Convention has occurred, it can require the State in question to cease the alleged violations, or even decide to exclude the offending State from the Council of Europe (Article 8 of the Statute). This decision would probably have been taken against the Greek government (which took power following the 1967 *coup d'etat*) if the government itself had not withdrawn from the Council in December 1969. In contrast, no specific provision is made for this type of sanction by the Statutes of the Organization of African Unity or the Organization of American States.

The specific competence in the field of human rights which the Council of Europe enjoys in its 21 member states provides its parliamentary assembly with a strong basis for extending its concern and expertise to other countries. The Council's role in the field of human rights is strengthened by the fact that many Heads of State and Heads of Government have chosen to speak on the subject during its meetings.

It should be no surprise that the elected representatives of the few parliamentary democracies existing in the world consider themselves particularly well qualified to voice opinions on the subject. They wish first and foremost to show their solidarity with those in many parts of the world whose fundamental rights are violated, and thus help bring about or restore democracy.

The European Parliament
In many cases, the efforts of the Parliamentary Assembly of the Council of Europe and those of the European Parliament overlap, in that the twelve countries of the EEC also belong to the Council of Europe. Some feel that this makes initiatives taken by the European Parliament superfluous.

Confirming the declaration of European identity, however, the Heads of State and Heads of Government of member countries as well as the institutions of the European Community—its Parliament, Council, and Commission—together made a solemn declaration on 5 April 1977 emphasizing the importance they attached to respect for human rights, the rights enshrined in the respective constitutions of Member States, and in the European Convention on safeguarding human rights and fundamental liberties.

The work of the Community in the field of human rights, therefore, has a solid legal and political foundation, upon which are based the rights of the European Parliament, which is elected by universal suffrage.

Regarding international relations, Member States have specifically recognized the competence of the European Parliament to monitor political cooperation with other countries. Since 1981, the President of the Council of Europe may address the European Parliament during his term of office in order to report on its activity. Action by the Parliament may take several different forms: members can address written and oral questions to the Chairman of the Council of Ministers or to the Commission, or meetings of the Political Commission of the European Parliament regarding the signature, the renewal, or the possible cancellation of agreements with third parties; emergency discussion in plenary session; or consideration of comprehensive reports on relations between the EEC and other countries. Since 1984, the Parliament has decided to present an annual report on human rights throughout the world, prepared by a Sub-Commission specially appointed for this purpose.

Statements and reports of this kind made by the Parliament are intended, firstly, to put pressure on the Council and on governments of Member States to impose economic or political sanctions. In the case of Turkey, for example, several proposals were discussed regarding the suspension of co-operation agreements pending the restoration of democracy there. A number of economic aid projects drawn up under the Article of Association between the EEC and Turkey were suspended following a decision taken by the European Parliament in November 1984, and are still frozen.

In other cases, resolutions may recommend an embargo on arms exports to countries guilty of human rights violations or, indeed, to dictatorial regimes. Their psychological and political effectiveness should not be underestimated: it can be measured by the vigour of the reactions they provoke from the governments concerned which are anxious to preserve their image in international opinion. Public statements of this kind, when they are made promptly, provide moral support for dissidents and for victims, and can also prevent further abuses, including disappearances.

The European Parliament has addressed governments over particular instances of disappearance, both individual and collective, on several occasions. The resolutions adopted concern Afghanistan, Argentina, Cyprus, the Philippines, etc. In one resolution dated 19 May 1983, regarding disappearances in Argentina, the Parliament 'protested in the name of the free peoples of Europe, whose indignation and horror it expresses', demanding 'full information from the Argentine government regarding the fate of disappeared persons'.[5]

The combined effects of appeals, exposure in the press, public statements, and discreet diplomacy sometimes bear fruit, although it is difficult to determine the relative impact of the various forms of interventions. Unless and until there is an effective system of law to ensure respect for human rights, at the international level, through sanctions or other appropriate means, the struggle against violations will continue.

Emphasizing the importance of regional conventions on human rights, the European Parliament expressed the wish that existing instruments, such as the 1981 African Charter on Human Rights and the Rights of Peoples should be endowed with greater legal force.

The Organization of American States

The Inter-American Commission on Human Rights of the Organization of American States (OAS) was created in 1959. Its mandate has become increasingly effective, particularly since the entry into force of the American Convention on Human Rights in 1978, which put the Inter-American Commission on Human Rights on a par with the Inter-American Court of Human Rights—the two main forums for the protection of human rights throughout the region. The procedures employed by the Commission include investigations, country reports, and the consideration of complaints filed by individuals alleging violations of the rights listed in the Convention.

Unlike the provisions contained in the International Covenant on Civil and Political Rights or the European Convention on Human Rights, the mandate of the Inter-American Commission entitles it to consider complaints filed by individuals without the express agreement of its Member States.

When the Commission receives communications concerning massive violations of human rights, such as disappearances, it carries out a fact-finding enquiry into the case involving hearings of witnesses and consultations with the government concerned. The Commission may also send a mission to the country in question to undertake an in-depth investigation.

In 1974, the Commission sent a mission to Chile to investigate the situation regarding human rights. With regard to prolonged preventive detentions authorized under martial law, the Commission noted that a number of disappearances had occurred. It recommended the creation of central registries listing all detainees. The government denied the facts. Although the Commission continued to note the occurrence of disappearances in Chile in subsequent reports, it failed to obtain any concrete results.

An obvious limitation of the Commission is that it is ultimately dependent on the OAS, whose political institutions alone are empowered to impose sanctions against offending Member States. Until 1978, the General Assembly of the OAS ignored all recommendations by the Commission for action against the practice of disappearances in Chile. It was not until the 1979 meeting in La Paz that the word 'disappearance' was first used by the General Assembly in its resolutions. The OAS could obviously no longer ignore a grave problem which had been widely aired at the international level, and which had spread to other countries in the region. The OAS therefore declared that:

> The practice of disappearances is an insult to the public conscience of this hemisphere. It is totally incompatible with our common traditional values, and with the declarations and conventions signed by the American States.

The General Assembly then urged States in which persons had disappeared not to introduce legislation which was likely to hamper the search for victims. This was an allusion to the law passed in Argentina in 1979, by which any disappeared person who failed to respond within 90 days to an appeal published in the press could be presumed dead.

The Inter-American Commission also approached the government of Argentina on several occasions to protest against the serious violations of human rights ocurring in that country. In 1979, after sending a mission of enquiry to Argentina, it published a detailed report strongly critical of the military junta. This report, which was submitted to the General Assembly of the United Nations in 1980, contributed significantly to raising international awareness of the problem. It was also a decisive factor in the renewal of the mandate of the UN Working Group on Enforced or Involuntary Disappearances.

In answer to the military junta which criticized the Commission for failing to consider acts of 'terrorism' concomitantly with human rights issues, the Commission replied that the responsibilities of its delegates did not include investigations into terrorism or subversion. These matters do not fall within the scope of its competence, its task being to enquire into acts attributable to governments. The Commission stated that:

> The violence used by terrorist groups had been more than equalled by the security apparatus of the State, which had given rise to serious violations committed with the aim of eliminating subversion regardless of all moral or legal considerations.... The campaign launched for the annihilation of subversive movements resulted, under the most appalling, cruel and inhumane conditions, in the disappearance of thousands of persons who today must be presumed to have died.[6]

The Commission also stated that, no matter what the circumstances, governments may not use methods such as summary execution, torture, detention under inhumane conditions, or refuse certain minimum guarantees of legal procedure, since such methods infringe fundamental rights such as the right to life, the right to personal integrity, and the right to a fair trial. 'A government which faces the threat of subversion,' the Commission declared, 'has no choice other than to respect the law, unless it is to resort to State terrorism.'[7]

The reaction of the General Assembly of the OAS to this report showed a change of attitude towards the problem of disappearances, a change essentially limited, however, to resolutions and recommendations. The strong political pressures to which the OAS is subject do not allow it to make full use of its potential in getting its recommendations implemented.

The Organization of African Unity
Apart from defending the right of people to self-determination and

pursuing the struggle against racial discrimination, the Organization of African Unity (OAU) has shown little interest in human rights issues in general. In its Preamble, the Charter of the OAU merely makes a brief allusion to the Charter of the United Nations and the Universal Declaration of Human Rights. The African Charter on Human Rights and the Rights of Peoples was only adopted in 1981, and was prepared partly in response to the violations of human rights which occurred during the 1970s, particularly in Equatorial Guinea, Uganda and the Central African Republic. The Charter has not yet come into force, having been ratified so far by only 17 States.[8]

The Charter could be an influential instrument for the protection of human rights in Africa. The rights listed in the Charter are substantially similar to those in the Universal Declaration of Human Rights and other international human rights instruments. One important difference, however, should be noted: the Charter contains no derogation clause enabling Member States to evade their obligations under a state of emergency.

It also differs from the Latin American and European models in that it makes no provision for the creation of a Court of Justice. On the other hand, the African Commission may receive communications from States without any previous declaration recognizing its competence. Communications by parties other than States, however, are subject to a limitation which does not exist in other instruments: the Commission may only take action with the approval of a majority of its members. The principal sanction which the Commission can impose on States which fail to fulfil their obligations is the publicity given by the Conference of Heads of State to its report.

The Charter is an important step in the promotion of human rights throughout the African Continent. Its ratification by the remaining States should therefore be encouraged.

The League of Arab States

The League of Arab States, established towards the end of World War II, created a permanent Arab Human Rights Commission in 1968. Its programme of work deals mainly with the situation of Arab populations living in the territories occupied by Israel. At the national level, the Committee has invited Member States to create national human rights commissions to act as its local partners. Unlike the Inter-American or European Commissions, the Arab Human Rights Commission is a political body.

The Commission is composed of one delegate per Member State. Each delegate has one vote, and decisions are taken by simple majority. The Commission has little freedom of action, and only the Secretary General of the League makes contact with Member States.

In 1981, the League adopted a draft Arab Charter on Human Rights. The rights and liberties it espouses are broadly similar to those proclaimed by the Universal Declaration of Human Rights, while retaining certain specific features such as the aspiration towards Arab unity. The Charter makes no particular provision for procedures designed to monitor its implementation.

The draft plan to reform the Arab League presently being prepared might be an opportunity to fill this gap. Short of establishing new monitoring procedures, it could at least strengthen and clarify the role of the Arab Human Rights Commission.

In conclusion, it should be emphasized that effective procedures at the regional level are necessary and complementary to the activity of world bodies. Eastern European or Asian states have not yet made any provision for organizations or procedures designed specifically for the protection of human rights. The Association of Southeast Asian Nations (ASEAN) created in 1967, now comprising Brunei, Indonesia, Malaysia, the Philippines, Singapore and Thailand and the Council for Mutual Economic Assistance (COMECON), created in 1949, consisting of ten East European countries,[9] are primarily concerned with economic and commercial co-operation.

Yet the existence of a regional economic structure should facilitate the establishment of procedures for the protection of human rights. Mankind does not live by bread alone; it requires the satisfaction of fundamental rights, economic, political, social and cultural.

The obligations of States in international law are clearly laid down. It is the means for ensuring compliance with them which are fragile, and which must be strengthened to make them less vulnerable to short-term political interests.

Notes

1. Resolution 33/173 of 20 December 1978.
2. Report of the Working Group E/CN.4/1985/15,p.24.
3. E/CN.4.1492, p.5.
4. Report of the Human Rights Committee, Supplement No.40, A/37/40, 1982, p.173.
   Paragraphs 1 and 3 of Article 4 state:
   §1: 'In time of public emergency which threatens the life of the nation and existence of which is officially proclaimed, the States Parties to the present Convention may take measures derogating from their obligations under the present Covenant to the extent strictly required by the exigencies of the situation, provided that such measures are not inconsistent with their other obligations under international law and do not involve discrimination solely on the ground of race, colour, sex, language, religion or social origin'.
   §3: 'Any State Party to the present Convenant availing itself of the right of derogation shall immediately inform the other States Parties to the present Covenant, through the intermediary of the Secretary-General of the United Nations, of the provisions from which it has derogated and of the reasons by which it was actuated. A further communication shall be made, through the same intermediary, on the date on which it terminates such derogation.'
5. Official Bulletin of the European Community. No. C/161/124.
6. Quoted text is not an official translation. OAS/SER/V/II-49, 1980
7. Ibid
8. States which have ratified the OAU Charter: Benin, Burkina Faso, Congo, Egypt, Gambia, Guinea, Liberia, Mali, Nigeria, Rwanda, Senegal, Sierra Leone, Sudan, Tanzania, Togo, Tunisia, Zambia.
9. Member countries of COMECON are: Bulgaria, Czechoslovakia, East Germany, Mongolia, Poland, Romania, Hungary, USSR, Yugoslavia and Vietnam.

5. The Role of Non-Governmental Organizations

If human beings are to remain, or become, civilized, they must develop, or perfect, the art of working in association.

Alexis de Tocqueville

At the international level, several non-governmental organizations (NGOs) have gained wide renown. Their efforts based on experience and expertise are often a valuable complement to the work of inter-governmental organizations. International NGOs constitute a crucial link between national agencies and inter-governmental organizations. Their flexibility and lack of bureaucracy often enable them to study more deeply the context in which disappearances take place and the role of the authorities in establishing and maintaining a repressive apparatus. They also provide moral and material support to those whose rights have been denied. Their independence, moreover, allows them to publicize the results of their investigations widely, so increasing international awareness of the practice of disappearances. In addition, their quick response is sometimes vital in pre-empting more widespread abuses.

Disappearances occur in a general climate of repression which often follows the proclamation of a state of emergency. Experience has shown that, while such a measure may be legally legitimate, human rights are frequently ignored in the process. NGOs can therefore help prevent disappearances from occurring by drawing the attention of the international community to the first signs of political repression.

Disappeared!

Amnesty International (AI)

Amnesty International is undoubtedly one of the NGOs best known to the general public. Since its creation, Amnesty has become widely respected for its protection of Prisoners of Conscience.

Amnesty International uses three different methods for dealing with disappearances. When the life or health of a prisoner is threatened, the organization may mobilize its Emergency Action Network. In this case, Amnesty immediately invites its members throughout the world to send telegrams or letters to the authorities concerned, requesting them to take concrete steps to assist the prisoner. Prisoners are frequently tortured or are victims of extra-judicial killings, or disappear by becoming 'non-persons', no longer in existence in the eyes of the judiciary. The Emergency Action Network can therefore help in the prevention of disappearances of this kind.

Amnesty may also entrust a particular case of disappearance to one of its adoption groups, which approaches the government concerned and asks for information. If a person has been killed, the group will ask for an explanation of the circumstances. Groups also maintain contact with the victims' families and provide material and moral support. They use various methods to exert pressure on the authorities, including sending letters regularly to ambassadors, to Ministers of the Interior, Ministers of Justice, etc.

Appeals to public opinion are one of Amnesty's favourite weapons. In 1980, for example, national sections of Amnesty International throughout the world organized a vigil for disappeared persons in Argentina. Thousands of names were read out in public, to show that the victims had not been forgotten and to heighten public awareness.

The organization also deals with cases of disappearance occurring throughout the world in its Annual Reports, which usually attract wide publicity. Editions run to over 80,000 copies, and are disseminated in six languages. Amnesty's range of publications also includes a report devoted specifically to disappearances.[1]

The organization maintains close ties with several inter-governmental organizations at both the regional and international level. It regularly provides the United Nations Working Group on Enforced or Involuntary Disappearances with information. It also provides evidence and makes its experience available for discussion of questions related to human rights which are dealt with in the United Nations system.

The International Federation of Human Rights (IFHR)

The IFHR was one of the very first non-governmental organizations to be created for the defence of human rights. Like other NGOs, it liaises with governmental institutions working in the same field. Most notably, it submitted a Study on Non-Recognized Detention and its Role in the Practice of Enforced or Involuntary Disappearances to the 38th Session of the United Nations Commission on Human Rights.

The IFHR has undertaken fact-finding missions in order to look into the general status of human rights in several countries. These missions include investigation of special situations such as disappearances in Guatemala (October 1983) and in Lebanon (January 1984). Legal information thus gathered enables the Federation to determine whether the accused have been granted a fair trial and enjoy fundamental legal safeguards.

The International Commission of Jurists (ICJ)

As its name implies, the activities of the ICJ are of a legal nature. It deals with issues of national and international law which arise from violations of human rights. The Commission has some 50 national branches which keep it informed of judicial activities in their respective countries.

The International Commission of Jurists regularly produces reports and organizes seminars on human rights issues. The former include, for example, a study on States of Emergency and their Impact on Human Rights.[2] The Commission also publishes reports on the human rights situation in a given country, such as those relating to Uganda (1974), El Salvador (1978), Guatemala (1979), and most recently the Philippines (1984). These publications all touch on the subject of disappearances.

The Commission also produces a newsletter, distributed worldwide, which reports on all of its activities. It frequently sends observers to attend trials and to determine whether the accused is given the benefit of due process of law. The presence of the Commission on such occasions, which the governments concerned do not always greet with enthusiasm, is a means of exerting pressure and helps to ensure respect for legal safeguards. It also reassures the accused, who knows that any deviation from a fair trial will have repercussions outside the country. The Commission indeed has no compunction in denouncing, in its statements to the press, violations, by the State concerned, of fundamental rules of procedure or other human rights.

The Commission also plays a very active role in debates on disappearances at the United Nations. In particular, it provides information on individual cases in a number of countries, covering the legal procedures involved and the remedies available.

The International Association of Democratic Lawyers (IADL)

IADL has a similar legal orientation. It undertakes studies on various human rights problems, and organizes symposia and conferences, also relating to democratic freedoms, peace, and international security.

Some of its reports are based on field missions undertaken to certain countries, including Nicaragua (February 1982), Turkey (April 1982), the Occupied Territories (May 1982), and Guatemala (January 1985).

The Association publishes a periodical, the *Review of Contemporary Law*, which contains articles and legal texts on human rights. Like the International Commission of Jurists, the Association denounces, when appropriate, human rights violations in particular countries. It also sends observers to attend the trials of political dissidents.

Together with the International Law Commission, the International Centre for the Independence of Judges and Lawyers, the International Federation of Human Rights, the International Movement of Catholic Jurists and the International Union of Lawyers, the International Association of Democratic Lawyers convened the Paris colloquium on disappearances in 1981. It also attends meetings held by the Latin American Federation of Associations of Relatives of Disappeared Detainees (FEDEFAM) and supports its activities. In February 1983, for example, it requested the UN

Commission on Human Rights to consider favourably the draft Convention on disappearances proposed by FEDEFAM. More recently, the Association approached the President of the NGO Conference and the Chairman of the Special Committee of International NGOs on Human Rights to consider the possibility of joint action by NGOs to facilitate the adoption of a Convention on disappearances.

The International Committee of the Red Cross (ICRC)

Unlike many other agencies, the work of the ICRC is based on confidentiality and discretion. It has been confronted with the problem of disappearances for many years. Its traditional role has been to intervene in international or national armed conflicts in order to assist military or civilian personnel missing as a result of hostilities.

Shortly after its creation, the ICRC established an information centre for the missing, the sick and wounded, known today as the Central Tracing Agency. Its role is recognized by the Geneva Convention of 1949, which has been ratified by 161 States. Over 50 million names have been listed in the Central Tracing Agency's archives since its establishment, and there is a constant influx of new cases.

The presence of the organization during armed conflicts is all the more useful since the United Nations Working Group on Enforced and Involuntary Disappearances is not, in principle, competent to intervene on behalf of persons who have disappeared as the result of war.

Contemporary armed conflicts are frequently of a mixed nature, which makes it difficult to distinguish whether the law applicable is one relating to armed conflicts (humanitarian law), or that which applies during peace time (human rights law). In this situation, the problem arises of distinguishing between 'missing persons' in the sense of the Geneva Conventions, and 'disappeared persons'. Governments frequently maintain that many of those reported to have disappeared have in fact been killed during clashes between security forces and opposition groups, and are, consequently, cases of missing persons and not of enforced or involuntary disappearances. The presence of the International Red Cross on the spot therefore meets a real need in terms of humanitarian protection.

Its activities, however, are not limited to armed conflicts. The statutes of the International Red Cross give the ICRC the right to intervene on humanitarian grounds on behalf of disappeared persons in situations of 'internal tensions and disturbances'. It has done so, notably, in the case of disappearances occurring in Argentina, El Salvador, Chile and Poland. Internal tensions and disturbances are described as situations of relatively short duration or sporadic armed conflicts in which the State uses the armed forces to maintain law and order, preventively or otherwise. Most mass arrests, political detentions and disappearances undoubtedly occur in these circumstances.

The ICRC generally proceeds as follows: for every country concerned, its delegation, which includes a staff member from the Central Tracing Agency, prepares a list of disappeared persons based on the evidence it receives. It then carries out enquiries into unresolved cases, and transmits the list to the authorities with a request for clarification regarding the fate of the victims. These investigations are undertaken at the request of the victims' families who, as much as possible, are kept informed of all the stages of the procedure undertaken by the ICRC. In 1976, the President of the ICRC personally addressed a list of 822 disappeared persons to the Chilean government. Many of these cases were later resolved after a series of local enquiries.

Although visits by the ICRC were originally limited to prisoners of war, its activities have long since been extended to include visits to political detainees. By so doing, it can determine whether the conditions of detention meet generally accepted standards. It may also help prevent disappearances from occurring in prison, as it is far more difficult to make a prisoner disappear once he has been visited by the ICRC and detailed information has been obtained about his case. Since World War II, the agency has visited over 300,000 detainees in some 75 countries, in situations other than those falling within the provisions of the Geneva Conventions. It would, however, be very much in the ICRC's interest to have stronger legal foundations, such as a declaration of fundamental rights applicable in all circumstances, for this form of intervention. Such a document would have to contain more concrete, detailed provisions than the 'core' rights from which no derogation is admissible.

ICRC's technical experience in searching for disappeared persons, which is acknowledged by the United Nations, could provide guidelines for all governmental and non-governmental organizations wishing to collect information and contribute in other ways to solving cases of disappearance. The Organization of American States has, for example, referred to the provisions in humanitarian law for the search and registration of protected persons and the transmission of such information. Its General Assembly has recommended that States 'establish central files on all persons placed in detention so that their relatives and other interested persons can be promptly informed in case of their arrest'.[3]

To the extent its mandate and the confidential nature of its activities allow, ICRC co-operates with many other non-governmental organizations.

In conclusion, non-governmental organizations have many points in their favour in pursuing the struggle against disappearances. They can carry out investigations, co-operate in exchanging and disseminating information, study the legal problems which arise, provide support to the relatives of victims, exert pressure on governments, and help increase national and international awareness. Governments are generally more amenable to investigations and monitoring activity undertaken by NGOs than they are to missions sent by inter-governmental organizations, which are carried out by representatives of other States.

Notes

1. *'Disappearances': A workbook*. An Amnesty International (USA) publication, 1981.
2. *States of Emergency: Their Impact on Human Rights*, ICJ, 1983.
3. Resolution adopted at the 10th Session of the General Assembly, 27 November 1980.

6. We Can Do Better

Justice is truth in action.

Joseph Joubert, 1842

The preceding pages have attempted to describe the tragedy experienced by those who disappear, who suffer inhuman and often brutal treatment, and are cut off from their families and the rest of the world.

Whether one is directly affected by disappearances as a relative, or simply an observer 'on the other side of the fence', the reaction to this inhuman practice is the same: it's outrageous, it's appalling, it's got to be stopped and those responsible brought to justice. Our indignation reflects a deeper awareness that fundamental human rights have been deliberately betrayed and violated. Such an awareness compels action. Our spontaneous solidarity with the victims is an expression of empathy and our desire to see society function under the rule of law and justice. Universal conscience of this order, multiplied a millionfold, is the foundation of natural law, for natural law is no more than the expression in legal terms of the sense of justice found in every individual. This sense has motivated law since time immemorial. Centuries ago Antigone's cry to Creon for the right to civil disobedience and the appeal of Spartacus to the slaves bore witness to it. The origin of our concern is not any one state or continent, for evil is contagious, and a spreading fire knows no borders.

The struggle to combat disappearances is hampered by the very nature of the phenomenon. It is far easier to contend with a visible form of repression than it is to resist an anonymous power which slips through one's fingers, acts in secrecy, and cynically denies its own actions.

Disappeared!

How can one strip away the mask, identify those responsible, point them out, and prevent them from escaping? How can the supremacy of law and ethical values be upheld, and sanctions be made more effective? Unquestionably, the task is stupendous and the goal ambitious. By comparison, the means for achieving it are slender. In practical terms, scope for action is narrowly circumscribed.

The relatives of disappeared persons have put forward the idea of an international convention against the practice of disappearances. This proposal is supported by several human rights organizations, who consider such a convention essential. At the Paris Colloquium of 1981, three draft conventions were presented, by the Human Rights Institute of the Paris Bar, by the Permanent Assembly for Human Rights in Argentina, and by the Argentine League of Human Rights. A draft convention was also submitted to the United Nations Working Group on Disappearances by the Latin American Federation of Associations of Relatives of Disappeared Detainees (FEDEFAM).

Some will say: what? yet another convention! What is the point of trying to use the law against forces which deny the very concept of legality, and which go by the principle that might is right? Proponents of such view forget that the law is a weapon, and a powerful one, intended for the weak to resist the strong who sometimes think that they can do without it.

At a different level, others question the usefulness of a purpose-built convention, in that disappearances are already forbidden under existing law and that several procedures for monitoring and protecting the integrity of the individual already exist. In their view, these mechanisms should simply be reinforced, since they fear that the elaboration of a convention may indirectly serve to institutionalize the concept of disappearances. Many are also concerned that such a process might be used as a pretext to avoid action on existing cases until such time as the text is adopted. Indeed, plans for new conventions have sometimes been counter-productive. Whatever the legal measures, the basis of legal protection and the means for providing it must be improved and the procedures used for obtaining convictions and imposing sanctions must be made more effective.

Strengthening Prevention

Imposing a state of emergency is not necessarily incompatible with democratic principles. Violations of human rights only occur when the state of emergency is abused or the law flouted. Use of the right of derogation therefore requires the closest scrutiny.

States which exercise the right of derogation must respect the conditions within which it can be implemented. In particular, they must immediately inform other States of the grounds put forward for doing so, the nature of the measures taken, and specific rights which are suspended. International bodies should have at their disposal the means to make known the cases where such notification is not given.

Another requirement is for an up-to-date list of countries which declare or rescind a state of emergency. Within the United Nations, such a list could be the responsibility of the Sub-Commission on the Prevention of Discrimination and the Protection of Minorities. Furthermore, the category of rights from which no derogation is authorized in states of emergency should be extended, and should include, in particular, the right to a fair trial.

To prevent disappearances from occurring in prisons, the authorities in each establishment should be required to maintain proper registers indicating the identity of every prisoner, the reasons for imprisonment and the exact date of arrest, the sentencing authority as well as details of release or transfer to another establishment. An updated national register of all places of detention should also be kept. Such preventive measures may also serve to forestall the occurrence of unrecognized detentions.

More effective procedures

International organizations, in their present or future form, should adopt simple and speedy procedures designed to match the urgent nature of the problem. These should include:

* Direct contact with the parties concerned;
* The designation of bodies which are empowered to act between formal sessions;
* The option for some cases to be given priority on the agenda;

* The option to intervene even before all national remedies have been exhausted.

It would also be desirable for the UN Working Group to become a permanent body whose existence is not constantly threatened. If it were not always subject to annual or biennial renewal, and had greater financial and human resources at its disposal, it could play a more active role, including publicizing its activities in the media of the countries concerned.

Improving the Rules Relating to Evidence

The secrecy surrounding the practice of disappearances and the bad faith of those responsible make it difficult to obtain adequate proof of the facts. Where proof cannot be obtained through legal investigations, eye-witness reports, or irrefutable evidence, greater weight could conceivably be given to circumstantial evidence. This could be based on the behaviour of States and would have consequences equivalent to those of objective proof.

The notion of circumstantial evidence may seem incompatible with certain fundamental principles concerning the rights of the individual, particularly the principle that the accused is innocent until proven guilty. According to many legal experts, however, this issue as regards States is more in the realm of political and ethical sanctions than legal sanctions. Inter-governmental bodies do not have judicial powers, and their decisions are applicable only to States. Furthermore, if the accused party is an individual, he or she is entitled to bring an action for libel against the author of the allegations. This course of action was taken in 1982 by the Chilean Ambassador to the United Nations in Geneva after he was accused of torture at a session of the United Nations Commission on Human Rights.

In this context, the authorities would be held responsible whenever it was established that:

* They have shirked their obligations over a given period of time;
* There is a manifest discrepancy between the facts of the case and public statements;
* There is proof of insufficient diligence in the search for disappeared persons.

Circumstantial evidence could also be considered applicable in cases where the authorities failed to keep a regularly updated register of detainees in all places of detention.

More Effective Sanctions

International agencies concerned with disappearances have very few means of imposing or monitoring sanctions available to them. Their decisions are generally ethical or political in nature, and are not legally binding. In short, the only real form of leverage they can hope to exercise lies in public exposure. This threat adds weight to their conclusions and recommendations. Consequently, there is every justification for developing this aspect of their work and giving it formal status.

Just as there are graduated penalties in penal law, so a graduated scale of public exposure could be developed and implemented by international organizations, such as the United Nations Working Group and other agencies having worldwide or regional competence. The degree of exposure or publicity given would depend on the strength of proof obtained against the authorities concerned, on the gravity of their actions (isolated cases or routine practice), and on their willingness to co-operate. The scale could thus vary between procedures carried out confidentially to full-scale public sessions in which the authorities and even the individuals directly involved are identified. The scale could also apply to the dissemination of documents.

Finally, as mentioned in Chapter 3, the organizations most appropriate could consider the establishment of an international habeas corpus.

Concurrently with political sanctions exists the question of penal sanctions against those responsible for disappearances. Persons concerned should be held responsible, on a personal basis, for crimes attributable to them. They should then be subject to the corresponding punishment as opposed to collective responsibility and sanctions. Several human rights organizations are in favour of such an approach.

In both the draft conventions submitted at the Paris Colloquium of 1981 and the proposals outlined to the United Nations Working Group by FEDEFAM, for example, the practice of disappearances was defined as a crime against humanity.

The Organization of American States and the Council of Europe, for their part, have also condemned disappearances as a crime against humanity.[1] This verdict implies:

* Punishing those who committed or instigated the crime;
* Inadmissibility of pleas made on grounds of obeying higher authority or military orders for reasons of state, or of national security, or under emergency regulations;
* That those responsible are to be judged by a competent court having national or international jurisdiction;
* That the acts in question shall not be covered by a statute of limitations;
* Exclusion of individuals responsible from amnesty decrees;
* Exclusion from refugee status and the right to territorial asylum for those responsible;[2]
* The inadmissibility of the rule of non-retroactivity.

Experience has shown that the notion of a crime against humanity and the structure developed around the concept in 1945 is very fragile. This was recently illustrated in France by the case of Klaus Barbie. The idea of a crime against humanity is ambiguous, and other concepts such as war crimes, crimes against peace and international crimes increase the confusion still further. The concept of crime against humanity has itself been challenged, since it does not take certain elementary principles deeply rooted in statutory law and common law into account, such as prescription and non-retroactivity.

Nevertheless, a concept with fewer historical connotations than a crime against humanity, such as lèse-humanity or offence against humanity, could be developed with appropriate provisions for its application.

The problem is that no international penal law exists at a sufficiently developed level. To be effective, it presupposes, in any case, the existence of structures which could ensure its implementation and enforcement. In this respect steps towards the codification of international penal law are currently being taken by the United Nations International Law Commission. However, in view of the difficulties involved in applying penal sanctions internationally, a more realistic approach would be to concentrate on prevention.

At the national level, the government of Argentina, for example, chose not to forget the past but, instead, to repeal the law of amnesty proclaimed by the military junta on the eve of its departure and to punish those responsible for disappearances. This action could not cause the grief and suffering of thousands of people to 'disappear'. But it was a response to what the Sabato Commission, appointed by the new government to enquire into disappearances, termed the greatest and the most savage tragedy in the history of Argentina.

The real value of what came to be known as the 'dirty war trial' lies in its being both an example and a symbol. Indeed, the Argentinian people were able to watch the conviction of the military junta on live television.

By taking this action, which he had promised during his presidential campaign, President Alfonsin hoped to restore public trust in the country's institutions, and show that the basis of democracy lies in respect for legality and not merely in the ritual of elections.

The government decided, however, to judge only three persons from among the military junta and others at the top of the hierarchy. Only five out of the nine military leaders were convicted, and even they were given unjustifiably lenient sentences. This prompted a wave of protest from human rights organizations. In their individual capacities, the relatives of disappeared persons have also instituted hundreds of different proceedings against the military authorities.

In Uruguay, the new government also passed a law rescinding the amnesty proclaimed by the former military government before its demise. The new regime in Guatemala, however, where some 30,000 to 50,000 persons are said to have disappeared in recent years, has yet to follow the example set by the governments of Argentina and Uruguay.

Struggle against Indifference to Evil

Indifference is the worst enemy of human rights. Today, perhaps more than ever, the world needs an immense humanitarian upsurge if it is to resist violence and the abuse of power—a form of madness known to be contagious. As the 20th Century draws to a close, we know that it should have given birth to a genuine Enlightenment, illuminated by the genius of Man. Alas, humanity is still threatened by vast areas of darkness. We must open our eyes and our ears, and break down the walls of silence.

To counterbalance the State and resist the use of violence, NGOs have great potential. Though weak, they can cause the strong to think again. They can keep a close watch on governments, challenge them and enhance public awareness by the first-hand evidence they provide. They serve as nerve-centres for information and action. Frequently threatened and perceived as opponents by their respective governments, those concerned with disappearances do not enjoy the international support which is forthcoming for NGOs working in other fields. Yet support is essential if they are to establish themselves, organize, compile records and publish information. The amalgamation of NGOs into federations, such as FEDEFAM in Latin America, would no doubt also be desirable for those in other parts of the world. The fact that the regime of a particular country no longer resorts to disappearances or brings some of those responsible to justice does not mean that the problem no longer exists. Unresolved cases will still need to be clarified. NGOs cannot afford to relax their efforts.

The press, with all the resources at its disposal, must draw the attention of the public at large to the hidden drama. In doing so, it must respect the truth scrupulously. If the national media are kept on a tight rein or are violently repressed for defying a government veto, then information on the problem must come from the international press. The world can no longer acquiesce in censorship.

In recent years, thanks to enhanced public awareness, human rights have become an increasingly important factor in relations between peoples and States. If this trend is to continue and spread, information must be made to circulate even more widely, through the written word, in books and articles, through radio and television, and through public meetings and debates in parliament. We should all be able to echo the words of Pascal: 'Knowing all this, I cannot sleep.' Public opinion must be kept constantly on the alert. If it is allowed to forget or become indifferent, we may lose one of the most effective forces for progress in human rights, and against the violence and periodic relapses into barbarity which can overcome civilization.

It is in awareness, of the individual, of the community, of society as a whole, that the greatest hope lies.

Notes

1. For OAS, see R. 66 XI-0/83. For Council of Europe, see Res. 828 (1984).
2. See Article 1 of the Convention relating to the Status of Refugees, and Article 1 of the Declaration on Territorial Asylum dated 14 December 1967.

   Also, Articles 3 and 4 of the 1968 Convention on the Non-Applicability of Statutory Limitations to War Crimes and Crimes against Humanity.

   In general, states are obliged to adopt all necessary domestic measures with a view to making possible the extradition of those responsible for crimes against humanity and to ensure that statutory and other limitations shall not apply to the prosecution and punishment of such crimes.

Appendix One: General Assembly Resolution 33/173

(Adopted at the 90th plenary meeting of the thirty-third session, on 20 December 1978)

Disappeared Persons

The General Assembly

Recalling the provisions of the Universal Declaration of Human Rights,[1] in particular articles 3, 5, 9, 10 and 11 concerning, *inter alia* , the right to life, liberty and security of person, freedom from torture, freedom from arbitrary arrest and detention, and the right to a fair and public trial, and the provisions of articles 6,7, 9 and 10 of the International Covenant on Civil and Political Rights, which define and establish safeguards for certain of these rights,

Deeply concerned by reports from various parts of the world relating to enforced or involuntary disappearances of persons as a result of excesses on the part of law enforcement or security authorities or similar organizations, often while such persons are subject to detention or imprisonment, as well as of unlawful actions or widespread violence,

Concerned also at reports of difficulties in obtaining reliable information from competent authorities as to the circumstances of such persons, including reports of the persistent refusal of such authorities or organizations to acknowledge that they hold such persons in their custody or otherwise to account for them,

---

1 Resolution 217 A (III).
2 Resolution 2200 A (XXI), annex.

Mindful of the danger to the life, liberty and physical security of such persons arising from the persistent failure of these authorities or organizations to acknowledge that such persons are held in custody or otherwise to account for them,

Deeply moved by the anguish and sorrow which such circumstances cause to the relatives of disappeared persons, especially to spouses, children and parents,

1. *Calls upon* Governments:
   (a) In the event of reports of enforced or involuntary disappearances, to devote appropriate resources to searching for such persons and to undertake speedy and impartial investigations;
   (b) To ensure that law enforcement and security authorities or organizations are fully accountable, especially in law, in the discharge of their duties, such accountability to include legal responsibility for unjustifiable excesses which might lead to enforced or involuntary disappearances and to other violations of human rights;
   (c) To ensure that the human rights of all persons, including those subjected to any form of detention and imprisonment, are fully respected;
   (d) To co-operate with other Governments, relevant United Nations organs, specialized agencies, inter-governmental organizations and humanitarian bodies in a common effort to search for, locate or account for such persons in the event of reports of enforced or involuntary disappearances;

2. *Requests* the Commission on Human Rights to consider the question of disappeared persons with a view to making appropriate recommendations;

3. *Urges* the Secretary-General to continue to use his good offices in cases of enforced or involuntary disappearances of persons, drawing, as appropriate, upon the relevant experience of the International Committee of the Red Cross and of other humanitarian organizations;

4. *Requests* the Secretary-General to draw the concerns

expressed in the present resolution to the attention of all Goverments, regional and inter-regional organizations and specialized agencies for the purpose of conveying on an urgent basis the need for disinterested humanitarian action to respond to the situation of persons who have disappeared.

Appendix Two: Information note on the Independent Commission on International Humanitarian Issues

The establishment of an Independent Commission on International Humanitarian Issues is the response of a group of eminent persons from all parts of the world to the need to enhance international awareness of humanitarian issues and to promote a climate favouring progress in the humanitarian field.

The Independent Commission on International Humanitarian Issues held its first plenary meeting in New York in November 1983. Its work is intended to be a part of the continuing search by the world community for a more adequate international framework to uphold human dignity and rise to the challenge of colossal injustices and humanitarian problems arising with increasing frequency in a modern world more commonly concerned with economic, political and military priorities.

Background

In 1981, the United Nations General Assembly adopted a resolution relating to a New International Humanitarian Order in which it recognized: 'the importance of further improving a comprehensive international framework which takes fully into account existing instruments relating to humanitarian questions as well as the need for addressing those aspects which are not yet adequately covered.' It was stressed that 'institutional arrangements and actions of governmental and non-governmental bodies might need to be further strengthened to respond effectively in situations requiring humanitarian actions.'

The following year, the General Assembly lent its support to the 'proposal for establishment, outside the United Nations framework, of an "Independent Commission on International Humanitarian Issues" composed of leading personalities in the humanitarian field or having wide experience of government or world affairs.'

In 1985, the United Nations Secretary-General presented to the General Assembly a comprehensive report and comments from governments on the New International Humanitarian Order. The report included a description of the Independent Commission and its work. In a subsequent resolution, the General Assembly took note of the activities of the Commission and looked forward to the outcome of its efforts and its Final Report.

Composition of the Commission

The Commission is an independent body whose members participate in their personal capacity and not as representatives of governments or international bodies to which they may belong. Its work is intended to complement, not to duplicate, work being done by existing governmental or non-governmental bodies, and to assist, not to interfere with, governmental negotiations or inter-state relations.

The composition of the Commission, which is intended to remain limited, is based on equitable geographical distribution. At present, it has twenty-seven members. The Commission operates through a small Secretariat which coordinates research activities and provides support services for its work. In its deliberations, the Commission benefits from the advice of governments, existing international governmental and non-governmental bodies and leading experts.

Programme of Work

There are, of course, many important subjects relating to humanitarian issues of relevance to contemporary society. With a limited mandate of three years, 1983-1986, the Commission has chosen three main areas of study, in which it feels its contribution can be particularly effective. These are:

* Humanitarian norms in the context of armed conflicts.
* Natural and man-made disasters.
* Vulnerable groups requiring special care and protection such as refugees and displaced persons, stateless persons, children and youth, indigenous populations, etc.

The conclusions and recommendations of the Commission are based on studies carried out with the help of recognized experts and national or international bodies chosen from all parts of the world for their specialized knowledge or experience. In addition to direct input by experts in the form of policy-oriented research papers, the Commission also sponsors panel discussions or brainstorming sessions. In order to avoid duplication of effort, complement ongoing projects and help promote innovative solutions, the Commission works closely with agencies already involved in dealing with these issues. Heads of these organizations or their representatives are invited to the Commission's bi-annual plenary meetings.

Studies and expert advice received by the Commission as well as its own delibertions on various issues are reflected in a series of sectoral reports which are published from time to time. These reports are addressed to policy-makers within governments, regional bodies, inter-governmental and non-governmental organizations and the general public. They are intended to be readable summaries of the subject, presenting an overview of the situation, prompting further research, making recommendations and suggesting concrete options for follow-up action.

The first sectoral report for the Commission, entitled *Famine: A Man-Made Disaster?* was published in 1985. The purpose of this Report was to increase public awareness of the famine conditions afflicting much of Africa and the Third World, recommend positive solutions and facilitate further study and analysis of the situation. The Report has already been published in eight languages, and the Commission feels that rather than waiting for the publication of its Final Report, the dissemination of these sectoral reports is a worthwhile exercise.

Sectoral reports on Deforestation, Desertification, Disappeared Persons, Street Children, Humanitarian Norms and Armed Conflict, and Refugees have been published in 1986. Additional reports on Indigenous Peoples, Statelessness, Mass Expulsions, Disaster Management, Urban Migration and other topics are forthcoming.

The Commission's work will culminate in the publication of its Final Report scheduled at the end of 1986. The Final Report will address the humanitarian implications of a diverse range of global issues. It will be a policy and practice-oriented blueprint for effective response to the tremendous challenge posed by humanitarian problems in modern society.

Members of the Commission

Sadruddin AGA KHAN (Iran) — UN High Commissioner for Refugees, 1965-77; Special Consultant to the UN Secretary General since 1978. Special Rapporteur of the UN Human Rights Commission, 1981. Founder-President of the Bellerive Group.

Susanna AGNELLI (Italy) — Under-Secretary of State for Foreign Affairs since 1983. Member of the Italian Senate. Member of the European Parliament, 1979-81. Journalist and author.

Talal Bin Abdul Aziz AL SAUD (Saudi Arabia) — President, the Arab Gulf Programme for UN Development Organizations (AGFUND). UNICEF's Special Envoy, 1980-84. Former Administrator of Royal Palaces, Minister of Communications, of Finance and National Economy, and Vice-President of the Supreme Planning Commission.

Paulo Evaristo ARNS (Brazil) — Cardinal Archbishop of Sao Paulo. Chancellor of the Pontifical Catholic University, Sao Paulo State. Journalist and author.

Mohammed BEDJAOUI (Algeria) — Judge at the International Court of Justice since 1982. Secretary-General, Council of Ministers, 1962-64; Minister of Justice, 1964-70. Ambassador to France, 1970-79; UNESCO, 1971-79; and the United Nations in New York, 1979-82.

Henrik BEER (Sweden) — Secretary-General of the League of Red Cross Societies, 1960-82; Secretary-General of the Swedish Red Cross, 1947-60. Member of the International Institute for Environment and Development and the International Institute of Humanitarian Law.

Luis ECHEVERRIA ALVAREZ (Mexico) — President of the Republic, 1970-76; Founder and Director-General of the Centre for Economic and Social Studies of the Third World since 1976. Former Ambassador to Australia, New Zealand and UNESCO.

Pierre GRABER (Switzerland) — President of the Swiss Confederation, 1975; Foreign Minister, 1975-78. President of the Diplomatic Conference on Humanitarian Law, 1974-77.

Ivan L. HEAD (Canada) — President of the International Development Research Centre (IDRC). Special Assistant to the Prime Minister of Canada, 1968-78. Queen's Counsel.

M. HIDAYATULLAH (India) — Vice-President of India, 1979-84. Chief Justice of the Supreme Court, 1968-70; Chief Justice of the Nagpur and Madhya Pradesh High Courts, 1954-58; Chancellor of the Jamia Millia Islamia since 1979. Former Chancellor of the Universities of Delhi, Punjab. Author

Aziza HUSSEIN (Egypt) — Member of the Population Council. President of the International Planned Parenthood Federation, 1977-85. Fellow at the International Peace Academy, Helsinki, 1971; the Aspen Institute of Humanistic Studies, 1978-79.

Manfred LACHS (Poland) — Judge at the International Court of Justice since 1967 and its President, 1973-76. Professor of Political Science and International Law. Former Chairman of the UN Legal Committee on the Peaceful Uses of Outer Space.

Robert S. McNAMARA (USA) — President of the World Bank, 1968-81; Secretary of Defense, 1961-68. President, Ford Motor Company, 1960-61; Trustee of the Brookings Institute, Ford Foundation, the Urban Institute and the California Institute of Technology. Author.

105

Disappeared!

Lazar MOJSOV (Yugoslavia) — Member of the Presidency of the Socialist Federal Republic of Yugoslavia. Former Foreign Minister. Ambassador to the USSR, Mongolia, Austria, the United Nations, 1958-74. President of the UN General Assembly, 32nd Session and of the Special Session on Disarmament, 1978.

Mohammed MZALI (Tunisia) — Prime Minister and General Secretary of the Destorian Socialist Party. Member of the National Assembly since 1959. Former Minister of National Defence, Education, Youth and Sports and Health. Author.

Sadako OGATA (Japan) — Professor at the Institute of International Relations, Sophia University, Tokyo. Representative of Japan to the United Nations Human Rights Commission. Member of the Trilateral Commission.

David OWEN (United Kingdom) — Member of Parliament since 1966. Leader of the Social Democratic Party since 1983. Foreign Secretary, 1977-79.

Willibald P. PAHR (Austria) — Secretary-General of the World Tourism Organization. Federal Minister of Foreign Affairs, 1976-83. Ambassador. Vice-President of the International Institute of Human Rights (Strasbourg).

Shridath S. RAMPHAL (Guyana) — Secretary-General of the Commonwealth since 1975. Former Attorney-General, Foreign Minister and Minister of Justice.

RU XIN (China) — Vice-President of the Chinese Academy of Social Sciences. Professor of Philosophy at the Xiamen University. Executive President of the Chinese National Society of the History of World Philosophies.

Salim A. SALIM (Tanzania) — Deputy Prime Minister and Minister of Defence. Former Prime Minister and Foreign Minister. Ambassador to Egypt, India, China and Permanent Representative to the United Nations. Former President of the UN General Assembly and the Security Council.

Léopold Sédar SENGHOR (Senegal) — Member of the French Academy. President of the Republic of Senegal, 1960-80. Cabinet Minister in the French Government before leading his country to independence in 1960. Poet and philosopher.

SOEDJATMOKO (Indonesia) — Rector of the United Nations University, Tokyo since 1980. Ambassador to the United States. Member of the Club of Rome and Trustee of the Aspen Institute and the Ford Foundation.

Hassan bin TALAL (Jordan) — Crown Prince of the Hashemite Kingdom. Founder of the Royal Scientific Society and the Arab Thought Forum. Concerned with development planning and the formulation of national, economic and social policies. Author.

Desmond TUTU (South Africa) — Archbishop of Cape Town. Winner of Nobel Peace Prize. Former Secretary-General of the South African Council of Churches. Professor of Theology.

Simone VEIL (France) — Member of the European Parliament and its President 1979-82; chairs the Legal Affairs Committee of the European Parliament. Former Minister of Health, Social Security and Family Affairs, 1974-79.

E. Gough WHITLAM (Australia) — Prime Minister, 1972-75; Minister of Foreign Affairs, 1972-73; Member of Parliament, 1952-78. Ambassador to UNESCO.

Titles on Human Rights

Permanent Peoples' Tribunal
A CRIME OF SILENCE
The Armenian Genocide
1985

Kimmo Kiljunen (ed.)
KAMPUCHEA: DECADE OF THE GENOCIDE
1983

Raymonda Tawil
MY HOME, MY PRISON
1983

Maurice Lemoine
BITTER SUGAR
Haitian Sugar Workers in the Dominican Republic
1985

Helen Joseph
SIDE BY SIDE
Autobiography of a South African Woman
1986

The Above titles are available in both cased and limp editions, and can be ordered direct from Zed Books Ltd., 57 Caledonian Road, London N1 9BU. If you are interested in a full Catalogue of Zed titles on the Third World, please write to the same address.

- Rationale/ altered "Reality people
  who carry out dissapearances
- Moral Exclusion